Teacher's Guide

EXPLORING German

THIRD EDITION

Joan G. Sheeran

Consultant
Wolfgang S. Kraft

EMC Publishing

ST. PAUL, MINNESOTA

Editorial Director: Alejandro Vargas B.
Developmental Editor: Wolfgang S. Kraft
Production Editor: Amy McGuire

Production Specialist: Parkwood Composition
Cover Designer: Leslie Anderson

ISBN 978-0-82193-485-2

© 2008 by EMC Publishing, a division of EMC Corporation
875 Montreal Way
St. Paul, Minnesota 55102
800-328-1452
E-mail: educate@emcp.com
Web site: www.emcp.com

Printed in the United States of America
20 19 18 17 16   3 4 5 6 7 8 9 10

Table of Contents

Introduction

Exploring German includes the following components:

· Textbook
· Teacher's Guide
· Workbook
· Audio CDs
· Overhead Transparencies
· Symtalk Symbol Cards

The vocabulary units (all units except 4, 10, 14, and 17) incorporate a variety of interrogatives and common linguistic structures. Once introduced, they are repeated, reinforced, and expanded upon throughout the remaining units. The main ones are:

Unit 1	Wie heißt du?	Unit 11	Was hast du?
	Sprichst du deutsch?		Ist Martina heute krank?
	Wie geht's?		Wie fühlst du dich?
Unit 2	Was ist das?	Unit 12	Warum?
Unit 3	Wie viel ist . . . ?		Was hast du an?
	Wie viel macht das?	Unit 13	Wie viel Uhr ist es?
Unit 5	Wo wohnst du?		Um wie viel Uhr . . . ?
	Wo ist der Garten?		Welche Farbe hat . . . ?
	Wie viele Zimmer gibt es in deinem		Welche Farbe(n) haben . . . ?
	Haus?	Unit 15	Wie ist das Wetter?
Unit 6	Wer ist das?		Welche Jahreszeit haben wir?
	Wer sind die Kinder?	Unit 16	Welcher Tag ist heute?
Unit 7	Was machst du? (*activity*)		Wann ist der Feiertag?
	Wie ist ein Pferd?		Welches Datum haben wir?
Unit 8	Was ist dein Beruf?	Unit 18	Wohin gehst du?
	Was machst du? (*occupation*)		Welche Sportart treibst du?
	Wo arbeitest du?		Was machst du gern?
	Arbeitest du gern?	Unit 19	Was kaufst du dort?
Unit 9	Was gibt's zu essen?		Wie viel kostet diese CD?
	Hast du Durst/Hunger?	Unit 20	Wie reist du?
	Was isst du?		
	Was trinkst du?		

Textbook — contains 20 units. Sixteen units focus on practical and functional topics of everyday life; the four others focus on geography, art, music, and literature. The vocabulary units include dialogues and information about grammatical structures and culture. Each unit contains a simple paired speaking activity called *Zum Sprechen,* another interactive activity called *Du bist dran!* that involves hands-on activities, and finally, realia-based activities called *Lebendige Sprache* (Living Language).

Workbook — contains a variety of activities (simple, paired, cooperative learning, TPR, and realia-based) and games (mazes, crossword puzzles, and word searches). These activities complement and expand upon the exercises in the textbook.

Compact Discs (CDs) — allow the student to listen to and imitate the voices of native speakers while following the text. They also provide the student with an opportunity to practice the pronunciation of words and respond to questions. In addition, the audio component contains a Check-up Listening Activity for each textbook unit, which is worth 20 points. The teacher may use it as a listening quiz or simply as a listening activity.

Teacher's Guide — includes an introduction, unit objectives, sample lesson plans for two units, teaching suggestions, the audio script of each textbook unit, a black-line master of each Check-up Written Activity (worth 20 points) and its answer key, and finally, a black-line master of the Check-up Listening Activity (worth 20 points), its teacher's script and answer key. The Check-up Listening Activity is actually designed as a listening quiz and may be used as such or simply as a listening activity. Finally, the *Teacher's Guide* contains the times of the individual units recorded on the compact discs.

Overhead Transparencies — are full-color, coordinated with the 20 chapters of the *Exploring German* textbook, and include illustrations that the teacher can use to reinforce and expand upon a topic. These overhead transparencies are ideal for classroom participation within a communicative setting.

Symtalk Symbol Cards — are used as visual cues so that students can express themselves in German following a sequence of illustrated art. In learning the meaning of each symbol, students will be able to say complete sentences from the very beginning.

To the Teacher

Goals of the *Exploring German* Series:

Exploring German is an exploratory book intended to help introduce the German language and culture to a beginning language student. It may be used in a variety of ways:

1. in a FLEX program, that is, an exploratory program which introduces students to a variety of different languages;

2. in an elementary school FLES program, that is, one in which a specific foreign language is taught over a period of several years;

3. as part of a formal 7th and 8th grade language course;

4. as a supplementary component of a first-year high school course; or

5. as a means for providing less motivated students some entertaining yet challenging material.

Exploring German is not a first-level textbook and should not be used as one.

The goals of *Exploring German* reflect the National Foreign Language Standards: communication, cultures, connections, comparisons, and communities. However, since the book and its components are designed to be an introduction and not a first year textbook, its main goals are understandably limited. Its primary goal is dual: the fostering of topical and functional communication and the cultural awareness of classical traditions and the patterns of everyday life. Its secondary goals reflect and support the remaining national standards. The goal of connections means reinforcing one's knowledge of other subjects through new knowledge gained through the study of the foreign language. In the case of *Exploring German,* reinforcement is made in the main subject areas of arithmetic, geography, weather, music, art, and literature. The goal of comparisons is being aware of the nature of one's first language and culture and then that of the new language and culture. Two examples are the presence or absence of noun categories and the forms of address in English and German. The goal of communities is the sharing of the new language and culture with others in the school setting and beyond. This goal may be evident in the student's participation in language clubs, cultural fairs, e-mail and postal correspondence with a German speaker, and interaction with local German speakers. It may be playing in a community-wide soccer game or making a German food specialty for one's family, participating in a community group or club, or attending a festival. It may simply be telling someone else about an aspect of Austrian, Swiss, or German culture.

The specific objectives of *Exploring German* are to:

1. introduce the student to current examples of everyday speech in a visual and realistic way;

2. allow the student to practice these examples through a variety of interesting and functional exercises; and

3. introduce the student to everyday life and to provide a taste of the art, music, and literature of German-speaking countries that form part of the greater cultural heritage shared by all people of the world.

Exploring German allows the student to use the target language from the very beginning. Its friendly visual introduction reduces student anxiety about the difficulty of foreign language learning. Each of the 20 units presents the material by means of a photo preview, a practical application, and at least one realia activity. The realia activity contains a variety of useful items that have been coordinated with the general content. This section offers expansion of the material covered and additional cultural information for further discussion. Finally, *Exploring German* helps the student to understand and appreciate his or her own language by comparing it to German.

 is used to introduce necessary information that culturally or structurally enhances the topics presented in the unit. These boxed entries may provide further discussion and cultural comments if the teacher desires it.

Unit Objectives

The learning objectives of each unit will depend on how *Exploring German* will be used: as the first stage of several years of sequential study or as a short-term introduction to the sounds and the *look* of this language and to the traditional and everyday culture of the Germanic world.

For Use in an Exploratory Course

How many (or how few) objectives will ultimately be determined by the teacher and the nature of the Exploratory Course. If all 20 units are presented, the student should be able to perform the following tasks.

Unit Number	Title	Objectives — Students will be able to:
Unit 1	Greetings and Expression of Courtesy	ask and give personal information introduce oneself and ask how people are doing
Unit 2	Classroom Objects and Commands	identify classroom objects follow classroom commands direct others by using classroom commands
Unit 3	Numbers	count perform basic mathematical functions relate numbers to geometric figures comprehend costs in a store setting
Unit 4	Geography	realize where one is in relation to the target language countries and continents locate cities and geographical features on a map recognize the influence of geography on economy
Unit 5	House	identify the rooms in a house identify different types of lodging
Unit 6	Family	identify family members and their relationships to one another and one's own relationship to other family members
Unit 7	Animals	identify animals say what the animal is doing describe animals as big or little
Unit 8	Occupations	identify common occupations, work roles, and responsibilities
Unit 9	Food	identify basic food and national and regional specialties identify a proper table setting wish guests an enjoyable meal
Unit 10	Art	identify major artists and their works express feelings about works of art view works of art more critically understand more fully the decisions the artist makes to create a work foster an appreciation of art
Unit 11	Body and Health	identify parts of the body and their functions say how one is and feels inquire about another's health and well-being
Unit 12	Clothing	identify articles of clothing say what one is wearing discern appropriateness of apparel

Unit Number	Title	Objectives Students will be able to:
Unit 13	Time and Colors	tell time understand the 24-hour clock identify colors describe objects in terms of colors
Unit 14	Music	identify major musicians and their works listen with appreciation to various types of music distinguish between different types of music
Unit 15	Weather and Season	describe weather conditions identify seasons relate weather conditions to seasons
Unit 16	Days and Months	identify days of the week and months of the year write dates in the target language relate months to seasons relate weather to months distinguish work days from holidays say when something happens identify the mythological origin of the weekdays
Unit 17	Literature	identify major authors and their works understand literary movements identify plot and themes in terms of major literary movements
Unit 18	Leisure and Recreation	name various leisure activities tell what one likes to do invite someone to do something
Unit 19	Shopping	name various places to shop tell what one wants to buy ask about prices say whether an item is expensive or cheap buy or decline to buy something
Unit 20	Travel and Transportation	identify means of transportation understand and react to expressions used in airports, train stations, and at bus stops ask for directions

For Use as Review in Middle or High School

Select units as an alternative review for material covered in your regular textbook. Assign the units and listen to the audio components. You may wish to have the class take the Check-up Listening Activity as a quiz or use it to provide additional listening practice.

For Use in a Basic German Course

The intent here is to provide functional activities for language acquisition and culture for those students who are not yet ready for a traditional grammar-driven textbook.

Lesson Plans

Two sample lesson plans are presented here. Lesson Plan 1 presents a language unit, Classroom Objects and Commands (Unit 2). Lesson Plan 2 presents a cultural unit, Art (Unit 10). These sample plans are but two of many ways to present the topics of *Exploring German* in a lively and meaningful way. These lesson plans are intended only as a guide. Variations, undoubtedly, will depend on your methodology as well as on the time frame of your particular course.

Note: Crossword puzzles sometimes contain phrase-answers. When this happens, the space between the words has been left out in the puzzle. For example, NICHTWAHR instead of NICHT WAHR. This is done so that the words fit the puzzle.

Lesson Plan 1: Unit 2 — Classroom Objects and Commands
Objectives:

1. have the student identify (orally and in writing) all the classroom objects, using the language patterns presented in the unit

2. have the student ask (orally and in writing) about the identification of classroom objects using the language patterns presented in the unit

3. have the student recognize the name of each classroom object in German when it is spoken by another person

4. have the student carry out a specific command (physical action)

5. have the student request someone do something within the classroom (orally and in writing)

6. read and write symbol sentences, and describe scenes or participate in a dialogue

Day 1

Presentation of the language. As you hold or point to a notebook, ask *"Was ist das?"* Then give the answer: *"Das ist ein Heft."*

Next, repeat both question and answer. Say the answer once again and have the class repeat it. Continue in this way until you have presented about half the objects introduced in this unit.

After each group of four objects, check for comprehension by asking individual students a question and obtaining a response.

When all the objects have been practiced, review everything orally by asking *"Was ist das?"* Allow the students to ask you this question, as they point to different objects. Let them work in groups of two so that they can practice the question and the various answers until they retain them.

Associative learning may be sparked by a word game that begins with an English cue to elicit a German response. The elicited response is then used to cue another German-related response.

English Cue	German Response	German Cue	German Response
paper	Papier	Papier	Papierkorb
			Buch
			Heft

Assignment:

1. Write neatly in German the name of each classroom object that you learned today.

2. Write the German names of six classroom objects. Next to each name, write an English sentence explaining how, or for what purpose, the object is used.

Day 2

Review. Practice the names of the classroom objects taught yesterday by asking questions rapidly.

Presentation of the language. The presentation used on Day 1 may be repeated to introduce the remaining classroom objects, if any, and then the supplementary words. Use student drawings on the board to identify selected words. Ask once, *"Was ist das?"* and have the students respond, *"Das ist . . . "* Then the students can continue asking and answering in pairs.

Similarly, say each classroom command and have students repeat. Then have a student give a command to another student, who then carries it out. Example, *"*Patty, *geh an die Tafel!* After Patty walks to the board, she gives a command to another student, "Dave, *mach das Buch auf!"* Dave opens his book, etc. The associative learning game will now be expanded to include all nouns and all commands.

Assignment:

1. Write the German name of each classroom object that you learned today. Next to it draw a picture to show what this word represents.

2. Write these commands: *Turn on the computer. Turn off the computer. Read the book. Speak.*

Day 3

Choices of activities:

1. Have students take turns being the teacher, presenting two nouns and one command to the class.

2. Have students do all or some of the exercises presented in Unit 2. Walk around to observe the class at work and to give assistance to those who need it.

3. Play word or picture Bingo. (Have students make a grid of 25 boxes, 5 down and 5 across. In each box they draw or write an object presented in Unit 2. You call out objects in German. The students will put an X in the corner of each identified box. The person who has five Xs in a row, diagonal, horizontal, or vertical wins. Have several prizes ready to hand out.

4. Have students listen to the audio CD and respond to the exercises.

Assignment:

Complete the exercises in Unit 2, if not finished in class.

Day 4 (optional)

Review all written work not yet checked.

Choice of activities:

1. Test the student's comprehension of the entire unit by giving the Check-up Written Activity for Unit 2 and the Check-up Listening Activity for Unit 2 (on the audio CD).

2. Evaluate each student's speaking ability and comprehension in this way: 1. Giving each student one object to identify by asking *"Was ist das?"* The student should identify the object by saying, *"Das ist ein/eine . . . "* 2. Giving each student a classroom command, have him or her carry it out. Since time will undoubtedly not permit each student to answer all the nouns and all commands, simply choose one unique noun and one unique command for each student. In assessing the speaking ability, you may want to evaluate both the word itself and/or the pronunciation. The activity will give you an understanding of what additional practice students need.

3. Introduce the Symtalk vocabulary for this unit. Call on individual students to "read" the symbol sentences in the first activity. Then ask students to write down these sentences. Next, ask students to describe the scenes in the second exercise orally and in writing.

Lesson Plan 2: Unit 10 – Art
Objectives:

1. identify the names of famous works of art and their creators

2. identify the characteristics of artistic movements or styles

3. develop an appreciation of art by assessing their own reactions to works of art

4. know some brief facts about the lives of the artists

5. read and write symbol sentences, and describe scenes or participate in a dialogue (Although this unit does not contain dialogues, you may wish to include the questions, *Was zeichnest du?* and *Was zeichnet er/sie?*)

Day 1

Presentation of the language. You may introduce the unit by asking the students to look at one of the paintings or sculptures presented in this unit. Then ask some questions that will require them to examine the work of art more critically. Some sample questions might be:

1. What is the general topic presented in this work of art?

2. Does this work show an outdoor or an indoor scene?

3. Is this work about people, places, or things?

4. Does the picture show something that you would find in the country or the city?

5. If there are people:

   A. How many are there?

   B. How do the people seem (happy, sad, angry, tired)?

   C. What are the people doing?

   D. Where are the people?

   E. How are the people dressed?

6. If there are animals:

   A. What are they doing?

   B. Do they look real?

   C. Are they pets, animals in the wild, or can you tell?

7. If there are no people and no animals:

   A. What kind of object is represented?

   B. Is it something familiar or strange?

   C. Is it useful and functional, like a potato peeler or a pencil sharpener?

8. What is the background?

9. What does this work of art tell you? What do you suppose the artist wanted you to know or feel, if anything?

Next, you may discuss how the artist creates his or her work of art. Some sample questions might be:

1. Does the artist use color?

2. Which colors dominate?

3. Are there more of the darker shades than lighter shades?

4. How is light used?

5. How are the subjects made to appear (easily recognizable or hard to define)?

6. Do you see geometric shapes?

7. Can you identify the kind of materials or tools used for this art piece?

Such questions may set the stage for a general description of the artist's style. You can now use the biographical information given to direct a general discussion about the painter's life, art, and the period in which he or she lived or lives.

Encourage student participation with praise and recognition. Remember that the responses you elicit reflect personal reactions of the students to a particular work of art. In such cases there is no such thing as a right answer or a wrong answer.

When discussing paintings, ask the students to imagine what it must have been like to live at the time or under the conditions shown in the painting, if it is a representational piece of art. Such discussions should increase their interest in viewing other works of art.

Assignment: Complete the written exercises.

Day 2

Check the written work.

Presentation of the language. Listen to the CD that includes the Unit 10 Check-up Listening Activity.

Allow the students ample time to react (either positively or negatively) to each work of art presented. Take a survey of how many people like each piece. What do the results say in regard to the artistic style preferred by the class as a whole?

Use the commands in the target language: *Geh an die Tafel und zeichne . . . !* Pick ten students to draw an item from each of the nine preceding units and from this one. For example, girl or boy (Unit 1), a painting (Unit 2), a number (Unit 3), a map of a country (Unit 4), a house (Unit 5), a family member (Unit 6), a horse (Unit 7), a mail carrier (Unit 8), a spoon (Unit 9), and an artist (Unit 10).

Day 3

Presentation of the language. Prior to the written quiz, quickly check the facts by asking:

1. Who can tell me the name of the artist from (name a city)?
2. Which artist liked experimenting with new materials or styles?
3. Which artist created (title)?
4. Which style of art is associated with the artist? (Name a specific artist.)
5. What is this style like? (Classical, Romantic, Modern, Expressionistic, Impressionistic, Abstract)
6. What do you know about the life and the career of this artist?

Introduce the Symtalk vocabulary for this unit. Call on individual students to "read" the symbol sentences in the first activity. Then ask students to write down these sentences. Next, ask students to role-play the dialogue with a partner. Then have them write out the dialogue.

Written Quiz on Unit 10: Check-up Written Activity

Teaching Plans for Specific Time Periods

The length of time needed for an Exploratory Course will depend on each school's calendar year and the flexibility of the curriculum. When time is very limited, it becomes all the more important to present a program that not only teaches the basics but also creates in the student an enthusiasm for and an interest in the target language and culture, in this case, German. It is hoped that the student will want to forge ahead and experience German in the broadest sense: to learn enough of the language so as to communicate with others and to understand a bit of the Germanic culture and appreciate some Germanic contributions to world culture.

For optimal learning, practice the Symtalk section over two or three days. For more information on how to teach using the Symtalk method see page 24.

If you find that three units are too many for a particular week, choose one vocabulary unit and one cultural unit. Speed up or slow down, depending on the students' abilities and your time factors. Feel free to go at a slower pace. Make sure students have enough time to role-play, draw, speak, write, and listen as needed for each unit. Also, you may wish to have students just look through the book at their own speed and stop at topics that interest them in particular. With limited time, you must decide which units you wish the students to learn actively and thoroughly, and which ones you wish them to go over more cursorily.

Suggestions for a 3- to 4-Week Course:

Because this time period is very limited, the material should be presented quickly and effectively in terms of creating interest.

Week 1: Unit 1 – Greetings and Expressions of Courtesy; Unit 2 – Classroom Objects and Commands; Unit 4 – Geography
Week 2 Unit 6 – Family; Unit 15 – Weather and Seasons; Unit 9 – Food
Week 3: Unit 10 – Art; Unit 14 – Music; Unit 16 – Days and Months
Week 4: Unit 18 – Leisure and Recreation; Culminating activities (crossword puzzles, guessing games, food sampling, music and dancing, guest speakers, games) and Testing

Suggestions for a 6-Week Course:

Week 1: Unit 1 – Greetings and Expressions of Courtesy; Unit 2 – Classroom Objects and Commands; Unit 4 – Geography
Week 2: Unit 3 – Numbers; Unit 5 – Family; Unit 9 – Food
Week 3: Unit 6 – House; Unit 7 – Animals; Unit 10 – Art
Week 4: Unit 15 – Weather and Seasons; Unit 16 – Days and Months
Week 5: Unit 14 – Music; Unit 18 – Leisure and Recreation
Week 6: Unit 19 – Shopping; Culminating activities and Testing

Suggestions for a 9-Week Course:

Week 1: Unit 1 – Greetings and Expressions of Courtesy; Unit 2 – Classroom Objects and Commands; Unit 4 – Geography
Week 2: Unit 3 – Numbers; Unit 5 – Family; Unit 9 – Food
Week 3: Unit 6 – House; Unit 7 – Animals; Unit 10 – Art
Week 4: Unit 11 – Body and Health; Unit 12 – Clothing
Week 5: Unit 13 – Time and Colors; Unit 14 – Music
Week 6: Unit 15 – Weather and Seasons; Unit 16 – Days and Months
Week 7: Unit 17 – Literature; Unit 18 – Leisure and Recreation
Week 8: Unit 19 – Shopping; Unit 20 – Travel and Transportation
Week 9: Culminating activities and Testing

Suggestions for a Semester Course:

Present a new unit each week. There should be ample time for all the activities. Choose from: *Du bist dran!* exercises, guest speakers, bulletin board displays by students, listening exercises on CD, map work, Internet research on various countries where German is spoken, musical selections, sampling of regional food specialties, and a story hour featuring classic German children's stories. Since motivation is a prime factor in an Exploratory course, you might consider giving a unit quiz after every second week, rather than every week. In that situation you could give the written or listening activities as just class work and not as a formal assessment. Allocate one week for each of the 20 units.

Week 1: Unit 1 – Greetings and Expressions of Courtesy
Week 2: Unit 2 – Classroom Objects and Commands
Week 3: Unit 3 – Numbers
Week 4: Unit 4 – Geography
Week 5: Unit 5 – Family
Week 6: Unit 6 – House
Week 7: Unit 7 – Animals
Week 8: Unit 8 – Occupations
Week 9: Unit 9 – Food
Week 10: Unit 10 – Art
Week 11: Unit 11 – Body and Health
Week 12: Unit 12 – Clothing
Week 13: Unit 13 – Time and Colors
Week 14: Unit 14 – Music
Week 15: Unit 15 – Weather and Seasons
Week 16: Unit 16 – Days and Months
Week 17: Unit 17 – Literature
Week 18: Unit 18 – Leisure and Recreation
Week 19: Unit 19 – Shopping
Week 20: Unit 20 – Travel and Transportation

Teaching Suggestions

Unit 1 – Greetings and Courtesy

Introduce the material on page 1, such as greetings, expressions of courtesy, questions, and miscellaneous words in small manageable groups. Have students make flash cards of cues that represent the vocabulary in this unit. Examples: the moon for *Guten Abend / Gute Nacht*, the sun for *Guten Morgen / Guten Tag*, a four-leaf clover for *Viel Glück*, etc. Use these flash cards to elicit responses in German from the students.

Ask students questions, such as "Who can tell me a German girl's name that starts with a B?" and "Who can tell me a German boy's name that begins with an F?" Then have each student choose a German name from the list on page 2. Write *Tag! Ich heiße . . .*" on the board for students to copy onto adhesive labels. With their own name tags, students can now introduce themselves and ask others their names.

Discuss names in general and nicknames such as *Nele* for *Cornelia*, and variations and diminutives: Johann – Hans and Hänsel, Greta – Gretel, Anna – Antje, Katherina – Katja, the old Catholic-inspired names for boys such as Carl Maria von Weber, Rainer Maria Rilke and male and female versions such as Leon and Leonie.

Explain about the need for formality in certain instances. One should say *"Guten Tag"* to Herr Müller because he is not a close friend or relative, but rather an adult who deserves respect. Call on the students to identify other such people from their school, neighborhood, and the community at large. When the relationship becomes more casual, the greeting *"Tag"* is appropriate. Then the students should identify a friend or a relative as someone with whom one has a close and familiar relationship. The use of *du* and *Sie* can be pointed out. Since *Exploring German* is designed for conversations for and about the younger student, the formal use of *Sie* appears only in dialogues with adults (Unit 20).

Unit 2 – Classroom Objects and Commands

Start this unit by telling students to keep their textbooks closed. Have them repeat after you the question *"Was ist das?"* Then take the two groups of nouns separately. Identify first all the feminine objects by saying, *"Das ist eine . . ."* Then take the masculine and neuter nouns by saying *"Das ist ein . . ."* Next, tell the students to open their books so they can see the words. Go through all the nouns once more. Then, ask one student to point to an object on the transparency and ask the question. Another student will answer it. Then that student should go to the overhead projector and select another object on the transparency. Continue this lesson until all the classroom objects have been introduced.

Sharpen listening comprehension skills. Using either the picture in the book or the picture on the transparency, name a specific item such as *ein Lineal*. Ask students not to say this word but instead to locate it in the picture by putting their finger on it. Do not ask for the English meaning. Instead, ask what color it is and where it can be found in the picture. Obviously, if a student answers these questions incorrectly, he or she has not learned or understood the spoken vocabulary word. Never dwell too long on any one word; maintain a lively pace!

Play *Simon Says* with the classroom commands.

Have students point, speak, and do something! Ask for three volunteers. Student A points to an object. Student B says the associated command. Student C carries out the command.

Examples:

Student A points to:	**Student B says:**	**Student C:**
a computer	*Schalte den Computer an!*	turns the computer on
his or her feet	*Geh an die Tafel!*	goes to the board
a pen	*Schreib: "eine Klasse"!*	writes *"eine Klasse"*
his or her ears	*Hör zu!*	holds a hand to the ear and listens intently
his or her mouth	*Sag es auf Deutsch!*	says something in German
a picture	*Zeichne ein Bild!*	draws a picture

Ask for a volunteer to tell someone to do something. Have the class evaluate the third student's physical response. Let the class announce its verdict by saying *ja* or *nein*.

Walk around the classroom, pointing to different objects. Ask, *"Was ist das?"* Remind students to give the correct indefinite article for each noun.

Reminder Notes

Die Klasse refers to a class of students. It is also a short reference to *das Klassenzimmer* or classroom.

A *Tafel* can refer to either a traditional chalkboard or to a dry erase board (*eine Trockentafel* or White Board).

A piece of chalk is *ein Stück Kreide*.

Unit 3 – Numbers

Have students listen as you say the numbers 1 through 10 in sequence. Then break up the sequence into pairs and ask the students to say them after you.

Challenge the students by asking, *"Who can say the numbers 1 through 10 without looking at the words?"*

Write an Arabic numeral on the board, such as 9. Ask a student to identify it by saying its German name. Then the student who answers it correctly may now think of another number to ask. Continue until all ten numbers are practiced.

As you introduce the numbers higher than 10, begin to add and subtract. When the students feel comfortable with all four arithmetical signs, have them multiply and divide in German. Do some examples on the board or on a transparency on the overhead projector.

Do some practical applications:

1. Have students conduct a survey to find out how many would like to have an ice cream cone right now. Ask one person to announce this number in German. Tell the class to imagine that five students have just finished eating theirs. Ask someone to say how many are now left. Vary the survey to ask who wants a particular flavor and give results accordingly.

2. Show the class an insert from the newspaper or advertising flyer. Ask someone to identify the prices of store items by saying the price in German. Ask another student to select the highest or the lowest price.

3. Ask how many students have pets. Have the students raise their hands. Ask someone to count all the raised hands and announce the result to the class. Then vary this topic by asking how many students have a specific pet such as a cat or a dog.

4. Ask students to identify by number his or her age, house number, telephone number, and number of sisters and/or brothers.

5. Ask students to compare numbers. Look at the number on the classroom door. Say it in German. Then say the number on the next classroom door on the left (or right). Is it higher or lower than your own number?

Test listening comprehension by giving students ten different numbers, one from each set of ten. Tell them to write the Arabic numeral for each number said. Examples: Item 1: *vier* (Student writes 4), Item 2: *dreizehn* (Student writes 13), Item 3: *achtundzwanzig* (Student writes 28), etc.

Reminder Notes

The currency of Germany is the euro *(der Euro)*. The plural form is *die Euro*. One cent is *ein Cent (m.)*. The euro contains 100 Cent.

Euro and *cent* are separated by a comma. *Die CD kostet 18,50.*

Unit 4 – Geography

With a globe or world map, introduce geography in general. Say which languages are spoken in many of the countries around the world. Talk about the families of languages, as described in the Introduction of *Exploring German*.

Ask students to open their books to Unit 4, page 42. Ask them to name the countries that border Germany. Have them repeat after you the German names of these countries and then the Austrian, Swiss, or German cities on the map. Tell them, *"Geh an die Landkarte"* to find a particular place.

Give clues to sharpen geographical awareness. Here are some sample questions you could ask:

· "Find a city that begins with an S."
· "If you wanted to take a hike in the mountains, where could you go?"
· "Name the country that is directly east of . . . "
· "If you wanted to spend a week in the city of Gstaad next winter, what would you pack and what would you do there?"
· "When you take the train from Köln and travel to Wien, in which direction are you going?"

Have students take turns reading the cultural material in Unit 4. Add any other facts you wish. Then have fun with it by conducting a quiz show, such as Jeopardy.

Unit 5 – House

After students are familiar with the names of the rooms and the dialogues, ask them to give responses to the questions *"Wo wohnst du?"* (answer can be the name of a city or type of housing or both) and *"Wie viele Zimmer gibt es in deinem Haus?"*

Have students form pairs for an association exercise. Give Student A a list of English cues associated with various rooms. Student A reads each cue and Student B responds with the appropriate place. Examples:

Student A reads:	Student B says:
bathtub	*ein Badezimmer*
refrigerator	*eine Küche*
flowers and shrubs	*ein Garten*
car	*eine Garage*
coffee table	*ein Wohnzimmer*
dresser	*ein Schlafzimmer*

You may substitute questions for the cues such as: "Where do you sleep?," "In which room do you wash dishes?," "Where do you brush your teeth?," and "Where do you serve a formal dinner?"

Give students white construction paper, markers or crayons, rulers, and scissors. Each student will design a dream house. One side will show what it looks like on the outside. The reverse side will contain a floor plan showing rooms and features labeled in German. Encourage students to be creative by drawing flowers in the yard or on the patio, and drawing some furniture in each room. When finished, each student should say *"Das ist mein Haus. Ich wohne hier. Das ist die Küche,"* etc. You might wish to have these words on the board so that students can look if they need to. Confidence building and having fun with the language are the primary goals of the lesson at this point.

Reminder Notes
Each German noun belongs to one of three gender categories: masculine, feminine, and neuter. Each category has its own word for *the*:

der (in front of a masculine singular noun): *der Garten*
die (in front of a feminine singular noun): *die Garage*
das (in front of a neuter singular noun): *das Haus*

If the noun is plural, then the definite article *the* is *die* (pronounced DEE):

die Zimmer – the rooms

You may wish to introduce the abbreviation *im* for *in dem*. It occurs for the first time in Unit 2 *(im Klassenzimmer)*.

The word *Garten* can mean yard, as well.

Unit 6 – Family

Review the question: *Wie heißt du?* Explain the words *dein / e* and *mein / e.*

If you like, introduce variations of this question, using *Wie heißt . . . ?* Ask, *"Wie heißt dein Bruder / deine Schwester?"* Model the answers: *Mein Bruder . . . Er heißt . . .* and *Meine Schwester . . . / Sie heißt . . .* As soon as the students understand the pattern well enough, have them ask each other the names of their relatives and say how many children there are in their families. Challenge them. Ask, *"Wie viele Kinder gibt es in deiner Familie?"* See if someone can attempt an answer. Do not worry about grammar. Just build up confidence by having the students speak in German!

Next, ask questions about a well-known family, such as the current presidential family. *"Wie heißt der Vater?,"* *"Wie heißt die Mutter?,"* and *"Wie heißt das Kind?"*

Unit 7 – Animals

On the first day have the students draw on paper large pictures of the animals. Each picture should be labeled on the back with the name of the animal, including the indefinite article. Students can teach themselves by calling on others to identify each picture. Have the students ask *"Was ist das?"* Other classmates can rate the answer: *"Ja, das ist richtig."* or *"Nein, das ist falsch."* Vary this activity by having the students draw on the board or overhead transparency or place their drawings on a felt board.

The students can act out the dialogues. First, for listening and speaking practice, play the CD so they can hear and say the words. Then assign three or four groups of two people each. Each group can present the scene between Jutta and Simon. Make sure to use props such as a pail filled with apples and a large picture of a horse. The rest of the class can critique the performances of each group. The mini-dialogues can be assigned to other students. If your students wish, they can change the names of the characters. Emphasize that in a theatrical performance the actors must pay attention to pronunciation, gestures, and expression. The students' drawings can be hung on the wall as a backdrop for this farm scene reenactment.

Unit 8 – Occupations

Use magazines and newspapers to find and cut out pictures to represent the jobs presented in Unit 8, for example, an electric mixer to represent the cook, a stamped and addressed envelope to represent the letter carrier, and a theater program to represent the actor or actress. One student holds up a picture while his or her partner gets 30 seconds (or one minute) to say *"ein Koch"* or *"eine Köchin,"* etc. A variation would be to lay all the pictures face down and ask each student to turn over the next card. That student has 30 seconds to give the correct answer. Winners who correctly answer within the designated time frame earn a prize. (Have plenty of prizes ready at all times!)

If you would like to expand beyond the *ich arbeite / du arbeitest* forms, alternate with *er / sie arbeitet.* Try using the 3rd person singular form and review the word *wo.* Then ask the students where the actor and the farmer work: eg, *Wo arbeitet der Schauspieler / die Schauspielerin, der Landwirt / die Landwirtin?* The students may recall the answers learned in Unit 7: *im Theater and auf dem Land.* Otherwise, allow the students to ask in German and others to answer in English. Example: *Wo arbeitet der Arzt / die Ärztin?* - In the hospital.

Ask what kind of education and job training are needed for certain occupations. Encourage your students to think about their own futures and career goals. Tell about some of the economic and cultural contributions of German-speaking nations. Assign students to find out about the occupations of such well-known people as Wilhelm Röntgen or Werner von Braun or Arnold Schwarzenegger.

Reminder Notes
The German school system provides an excellent vocational education program. Students combine class work with actual on-the-job training. A vocational school is called a *Berufsschule.* Note: *die Arbeit:* work; *die Arbeitsstelle:* job, position of employment

Unit 9 – Food

Begin this unit with a discussion of American food specialties and what the class considers typical American food. Emphasize a tolerant attitude toward unfamiliar foods. Reinforce the idea that a food that one finds distasteful at first may later become quite acceptable. Lastly, remind the students that a food that one person loves another person may dislike.

Practice the vocabulary items by playing the word chain. Ask *"Was gibt es zu essen?"* Student A answers by naming one item, *"Es gibt Bananen."* Student B repeats what Student A says and adds another food. *"Es gibt Bananen und Tomaten."* You could expand this lesson by introducing the indefinite articles if you prefer. Or very simply, ask the students to say only a noun. Keep going until the last student can repeat all the previous words before adding the final word. To the winner of this heroic feat give a banana or a pear!

Do word associations: Have students name in German a food or beverage associated with or used to make a certain dish or menu. Examples: milk shake *(Milch);* a sandwich *(Brot);* spaghetti sauce *(Tomaten);* a sundae *(Eis);* Waldorf, Caesar or fruit, types of . . . *(Salat);* omelette *(Eier);* and fudge *(Schokolade).*

Make dinner menus. Each student selects a beverage, a meat, two vegetables, and a dessert and indicates a price for each item or a set price for the entire menu. This can be done orally or on paper.

Ask if any of the students have already tasted one of the specialties listed in the textbook. Perhaps some have eaten *Bratwurst* at German heritage fairs. Ask who has ever eaten *Müsli* or *Marzipan*. Ask them to look in their supermarkets for food products from German-speaking countries (chocolates by *Tobler* or *Lindt* or soups by *Maggi* or *Knorr*). Have volunteers tour the supermarket and write down as many products as they can find that have been exported from Switzerland, Austria, or Germany.

Reminder Notes

Guten Appetit! is a wish on the part of a friend or host for all guests to enjoy the meal and eat heartily.

Die Küche can refer to the kitchen or to cooking or food in general, such as in *ländliche Küche*.

Traditionally the large mid-day meal has several courses, often starting with soup and ending with cheese. Most people today, however, are not at home at this time. They eat out or take a bag lunch.

Evening meals are served at a time when the whole family can sit down together.

The noun *das Essen* means "food." The verb *essen* means "to eat."

Unit 10 – Art

Introduce this unit by asking students to think about the many different ways people decorate their homes. Talk about porcelain figurines, collectable plates, oil paintings, watercolors, woven wall hangings, family photographs, posters, mobiles, framed certificates, etc.

Give the students some questions to discuss, such as "Should a painting be like a photograph, showing exact detail, or may it be abstract or not true-to-life?," "Does a work of art ever convey some kind of message to the viewer?," and "Do you think artists should focus only on pretty subjects?"

To demonstrate different styles, ask two volunteers who feel rather artistically inclined to draw a duck on the board. You will most likely see two different versions of what a duck looks like.

Ask the students to look at the paintings in the textbook. Ask about artistic style. "Do you see a difference in the styles of all the painters?," "Which painting is the clearest?," "Which appears fuzzy or not true-to-life?," and "Which artist creates a lot of detail?"

Ask for volunteers to read the biographical sketches of the artists.

Provide bonus points to those who can obtain research on the following artists: Hans Holbein, the Elder (Renaissance painter 1465–1524), Johann H.W. Tischbein (portrait painter 1751–1829), Karl Friedrich Schinkel (painter and architect 1781–1841), Carl Spitzweg (Biedemeier painter 1808–1885), Käthe Kollwitz (Expressionist painter 1867–1945), Max Liebermann (Impressionist painter 1847–1935), Max Ernst (Expressionist painter 1891–1976), and German-Americans Albert Bierstadt (1830–1902) and Thomas Nast (illustrator of "Santa Claus" and the donkey and the elephant as political symbols 1840–1902).

Write on the board the names of all the artists featured in this unit. Survey student preferences by having each one put a checkmark under the name of his or her favorite work of art. Determine which painting or work is the most popular with your class and why.

Additional Activities

You may use these discussion prompts for the art in this unit.

1. *The Young Hare.* Does the hare look real? Can you see his whiskers? How are his ears drawn? Is the brown a solid color or are there varying shades of brown? Where is there a patch of white? On which side is his shadow? How does the artist sign this water color?

2. *Saint Anthony.* What is Saint Anthony wearing? Does he have shoes on? What is he holding? What can you say about physical location of the town? Can you identify any distinctive features? Do you see water? Are there other people? When was this picture made?

3. *Ships in the Harbor of Greifswald.* What object seems to connect the sky and the water? What two colors form the middle layer of sky? Is the sun rising or setting? Are the fishermen repairing their nets? Can you imagine the ship setting sail? What kind of mood does the artist create?

4. *Lone Tree.* What suggests that a storm has taken place? What is unusual about the top of the tree? Who is standing under the tree? Where are the darker shades? What colors show that the rain has stopped and that the sun is coming out? What part of the tree is silhouetted against the backdrop of emerging light? Does this picture convey an optimistic or a pessimistic outlook?

5. *Women on the Street.* How are the people dressed? Do they appear poor or rich? Do the women look happy? Are they walking toward you or away from you? What is the main color? Do you see anything in the background? What, if anything, is the artist is trying to say?

6. *The Large Blue Horses.* Are the horses being controlled by a human being? What kind of colors gives this scene a sense of strength and excitement? What major color is associated with the freedom of outdoors and open spaces? What do the horses seem to be doing? Does that convey rest or action?

7. *Mein kleiner Freund II.* Does this scene look like a photograph? Find two things about the child that are not natural and proportional. Would you rather see more realism and less fantasy? What does the image say about the relationship between the child and the cat? What is the background? What decorative touches add to the charm?

8. *Schatzkasten.* A traditional treasure chest contains jewels. This treasure chest contains our planet's best jewel. What is it? But why has the artist made it to look dried out and useless? What is the sculptor's message to the guardians of the earth?

Unit 11 – Body and Health

Review the question *"Was ist das?"* (Unit 2) as students are learning the names of body parts. Point out that the question *"Was hast du?"* literally means "What do you have?" and indicates ownership or possession as well as the expression "What's wrong with you?"

As you ask the question *"Was ist das?"* point to different body parts on dolls or pictures. Elicit the answer *"Das ist der / die / das . . . "*

Review the question *"Wie geht's?"* (Unit 1) and expand this topic with health-related expressions.

Review the interrogative pronoun *"Wer"* (Unit 6). Now ask, *"Wer hat die Grippe?,"* *"Wer hat Kopfweh?,"* *"Wer ist traurig?,"* and *"Wer ist gesund?"*

Perform short role plays. Have the students memorize the short dialogues and act them out.

Unit 12 – Clothing

To help students learn the vocabulary presented in this unit fairly quickly, give them hints such as "This article of clothing is to be worn outside. It begins with the letter J." *(Jacke)*

Supply students with the names of some hot weather clothing. Ask, "What should I pack for my (summer, fall, winter, or spring) trip to a specific place, e.g., Bern in Switzerland or Salzburg in Austria?" Vary the seasons and the destinations.

Do word associations. Student A mentions a part of the body, while Student B responds with an article of clothing associated with that body part. Examples:

Student A says:	**Student B responds:**
der Hals	*die Krawatte*
die Füße	*die Schuhe*
die Beine	*die Hose*
die Hände	*die Handschuhe*

Unit 13 – Time and Colors

Combine colors and classroom objects. Point to an object, such as a book, and ask: *"Welche Farbe hat das Buch?"* Students should answer with the German name for the color of the book: *"Das Buch ist blau."* After you have covered four or five objects, let the students continue on their own. One student asks the question, another answers. You may wish to extend the exercise by using articles of clothing or miscellaneous items in English, such as a valentine, a frog, a sunflower, water in a swimming pool, a strawberry, a snowball, a tree trunk, and a carrot. You may want to ask about multiple colors of one object: *"Welche Farben hat der Hut? (Der Hut ist gelb und schwarz.)"*

You also might try: "I see something *rot. Was ist das?"* For identifying objects not taught yet, students may use English, of course.

To check students' comprehension of the 24-hour clock, write various times on the board or overhead transparency (for example, 2 P.M., 10:45 P.M.) and have them say or write the equivalent times the 24-hour clock. Tell them to start with 12 noon and add the P.M. time (e.g., 12 + 2 = 14 o'clock; 12 + 10:45 = 22:45 o'clock). Transportation in many parts of the world operates on official time, which has a twenty-four hour basis. Official time is often used by schools, radio and television stations, and theaters.

Ask students to help create a list of daily or weekly activities, such as brushing teeth, carrying out the trash, or playing the piano. When you have about 25 different activities, have a student guess a number from 1 to 25. If he guesses number 12 (go to German class), then he must say at what time he carries out that activity. For example, *um Viertel vor zehn Uhr.*

Vary this activity using the 24-hour clock. Have students make a numbered list of 15–20 television shows or radio programs. Go around the room having students pick a number on the list. If a student selects number 16, for example, then he or she has to say in German the official time of the number 16 broadcast: *Das Programm ist um siebzehn Uhr.*

Unit 14 – Music

The traditional composers presented in this unit represent three distinct musical styles: Baroque, Classical, and Romantic. Play excerpts of famous music from each musical style on a CD player. Get some harpsichord music (a *Brandenburg Concerto)* and let the students hear the sound of this instrument. Play a minuet by Mozart and have them listen to 18th century dance music. For a taste of Romantic music, try a portion of Beethoven's *Pastoral Symphony (#6)* and ask students to listen for the sounds of a folk dance, a storm, and birds.

After the class has read the biographical sketches of each composer, conduct interviews. Ask for three students to act as interviewers and three volunteers to play Bach, Mozart, and Beethoven. Others in the class should contribute questions to be asked of each composer. (Of course, be sure to look their questions over first and check for inappropriate language.) The questions should give each composer an opportunity to say something about his life and musical accomplishments. Other students might enjoy making stage props for the interview scene and creating nametags for each of the interviewees, e.g., *"Ich heiße Johann Sebastian Bach."* Someone else in the class might wish to introduce this show as follows:

Es ist 20.00 Uhr. Die Musikstunde beginnt. Unser Gast ist Johann Sebastian Bach. Guten Abend, Herr Bach!

Help students who might like to try Internet research to find some audio samples of current popular musicians and groups, for example, the singers Peter Licht and *Sportfreunde Stiller.*

Unit 15 – Weather and Seasons

Start this unit by showing a globe. Remind the students that the tilting of the earth either toward or away from the sun results in the different seasons in the two hemispheres. Explain also that temperate climates have four seasons, while tropical climates have two, rainy and dry.

After you introduce the expressions of weather and seasons, ask the students to talk about today's weather and the weather conditions associated with each of the four seasons.

Have the students make flash cards that represent various weather conditions. Turn them face down. Ask each student to turn one over and then say in German what weather activity is suggested by that picture. It is certainly all right if more than one student makes a picture of the same weather condition. For example, to depict *Es schneit*, Student A might draw a single snowflake; Student B might draw a snowy sky; and Student C might draw a snow shovel.

Name a series of English cues associated with certain weather conditions and ask students to identify the weather.

Examples:

You say:	Students respond:
umbrella	*Es regnet.*
skis	*Es schneit.*
kite	*Es ist windig.*
suntan lotion	*Es ist sonnig.*

Reminder Notes

Notice the noun forms of some verbs:
der Donner = *thunder* → Es donnert. = *It's thundering.*
der Blitz = *lightning* → Es blitzt. = *It's lightning.*
der Regen = *rain* → Es regnet. = *It's raining.*
der Schnee = *snow* → Es schneit. = *It's snowing.*
die Sonne = *sun* → Die Sonne scheint. = *The sun is shining.*

Unit 16 – Days and Months

When students can recognize and say the days of the week and are familiar with the mythological derivations, ask them such questions as "Which day was originally dedicated to the goddess Freia?," "Which day is associated with the harvest?," etc. Make vocabulary calendars. Distribute to each student a large piece of construction paper, a pencil, a ruler, and a colored marker. Each student should create a calendar of the current month, labeling the month and each weekday in German. In each numbered box the student should write a different German vocabulary word. The words may relate to one theme (for example Animals, Unit 7), or they may be selected from different units. These calendars can serve as unit reviews whereby students can guess the words written by their classmates. If decorated and even colorfully illustrated, they become handsome wall displays.

Birthdays: Have each student say when his or her birthday is: *"Ich habe am 22. Oktober Geburtstag."*

Unit 17 – Literature

Begin this unit by naming some famous literary works such as *Little Women, The Wizard of Oz, The Little Prince, Heidi,* and the fairy tales collected by the Grimm Brothers and those written by Hans Christian Andersen. Ask the students what they are currently reading for fun. Ask how many have read a Harry Potter novel or to name a favorite story or author.

Ask students if they know that the stories *Bambi* and *The Nutcracker* were originally written in German. Show them some current books for young people that are written in German. (Karin Gündisch and Cornelia Funke are contemporary authors of popular books for young people.) Play story hour and read a simple German text out loud. Encourage the students to read in English and, as they progress in their language studies, in German. Find some German language comic books that might spark an interest in reading.

Have interested students gather more biographical information about the authors presented in Unit 17.

Unit 18 – Leisure and Recreation

Ask students to make flash cards that represent the first group of nouns presented in this unit: museum, beach, party, and picnic. Then point to each flash card and ask, *"Wohin gehst du?"* Model the response, *"Ich gehe . . . "* Continue asking and modeling the responses until the students can do both with no help from you.

Ask five volunteers to draw on the board the following balls: a volleyball, a tennis ball, a soccer ball, a baseball, a basketball, and an American football. One person points to drawing number 1 and asks the question *"Welche Sportart treibst du?"* (indicating that the answer should be the sport suggested by that picture). Continue until all balls and sports are identified. Then the students should try speaking freely by asking each other about their interests.

Relate seasons to sports. Ask, *"In welcher Jahreszeit spielst du . . . ? (Tennis,* etc.)*"* Do the same for the other sports. Take a class survey that shows when and what the students play.

Have students cut out pictures from magazines that represent the following activities: reading, swimming, biking, horseback riding, dancing, playing a game, and skiing. Lay them face down and have each student, one by one, uncover a picture and say *"Ich . . . gern."*

Unit 19 – Shopping

Have students form groups of three, with one student in each group playing the role of a customer, another student in the role of a salesclerk, and another in the role of a cashier. Each group should act out a simple transaction, with the customer asking the price of an item, the salesclerk telling the price, and the cashier ringing up the sale and returning change to the customer.

Reminder Notes
The euro *(der Euro,* singular; *die Euro,* plural*)* is the currency of Germany, Austria, and most members of the European Union. Switzerland and Liechtenstein use the Swiss franc *(der Franken,* singular, *die Franken,* plural.)

Unit 20 – Travel and Transportation

Look through magazines to find pictures of an airplane, a train, a ship, a car, and a bus. Point to one of the pictures and ask, *"Wie reist du?"* Model the answer, *"Ich reise mit dem Flugzeug."* Eventually students should be able to do this by themselves. Have them try to imitate a vehicle by waving arms to mimic flying or rowing a boat to indicate ship or hands on a make-believe steering wheel to suggest riding in a car.

Point out that the verb *reisen* may be used with all forms of transportation. The verb *fahren,* on the other hand, may not be used when referring to air travel.

Point out the use of formal address between employees and the public, and between strangers. (See note to teacher in Unit 1 of Teaching Suggestions.)

Have students form pairs and role-play a traveler purchasing a ticket from an employee at a train station or an airport.

General Suggestion
An effective way to introduce new vocabulary words and expressions is to use visual cues, flash cards, and the transparencies with and without the vocabulary overlays.

Reminder Notes
Travel vocabulary often offers you some variation. For example, in English you may say "I travel by plane," or you may say "I fly." So, too, in German.

fliegen   to fly
Ich fliege.   I fly.

Symtalk Activities

The Symtalk method teaches students the fundamentals of the target language through visual symbols that represent nouns, verbs, prepositions, and other parts of speech. Students learn to associate a word or expression in the target language with its symbol, which they then translate into speech and written expression. You will find that, with the first Symtalk lesson, your students will be able to speak in complete sentences in the target language.

The Symtalk activities in *Exploring German* recycle the vocabulary throughout the book, resulting in mastery of the core vocabulary by Unit 20. You will notice that some vocabulary in Symtalk is recycled from earlier sections in the unit, while other vocabulary—designed to expand students' oral expression—is completely new. Verbs are introduced as lexical items, so students learn conjugations naturally. There are three Symtalk activities, or exercises, in each unit. New symbols are introduced before each activity. In the first activity, students write the word or phrase under the symbol card. In the second activity, students "read" the symbols to create sentences. They should read the sentences aloud and then write them out. In the third activity, in most cases, students work with a partner to complete a dialogue using the new vocabulary for the unit. After expressing themselves orally, students again have the opportunity for written practice. They will be asked to write out the conversation they have just practiced orally. (Sometimes the second activity has students describe a scene rather than engage in a dialogue.)

Students will meet six Symtalk characters, who will perform many of the actions described in the activities:

Daniel   Brigitte   Thomas   Silvia   Anton   Hiko

Activity 1, Day 1: Reading Sentences

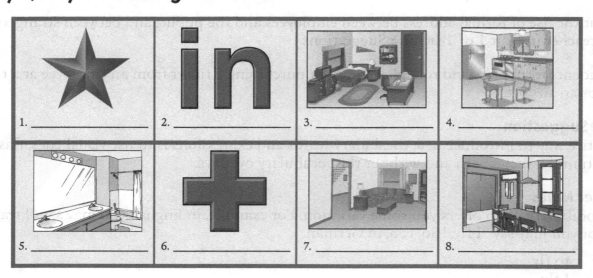

1. _____   2. _____   3. _____   4. _____

5. _____   6. _____   7. _____   8. _____

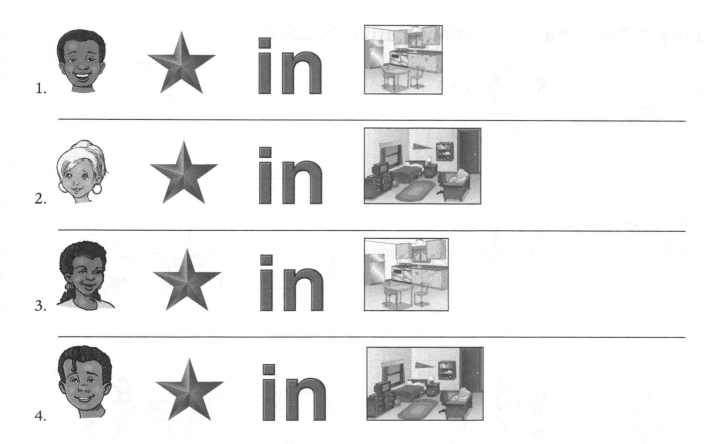

1.

2.

3.

4.

Begin by reviewing the names of the Symtalk characters with your class; ask students to pronounce their names after you. Then point to the symbol "is," and say it aloud in the target language. Ask the students to repeat it after you. Then do the same for "in the" and "bedroom." Next, point to one of the characters and say, in the target language, that he or she is in the bedroom and have students repeat after you, for example, *Silvia ist in dem Schlafzimmer.* If you have a set of the symbol cards that go with the *Exploring German* textbook, place the symbols for *Silvia, ist, in dem* and *Schlafzimmer* in a row on the board to form the sentence and ask students to repeat after you. Finally, introduce "dining room" and "bathroom" (masculine or neuter nouns), using the names of other characters to form complete sentences. Do the same for a feminine noun: "in" (*in der*) and "kitchen" *(Küche). Silvia ist in der Küche.* Once you are satisfied that students can orally reproduce the vocabulary and form sentences, write the spelling of the words in the target language on the board and tell the class to write them in their books underneath the symbols. (Sometimes there will be a singular and a plural verb form, which necessitates two blanks under a symbol.)

After you are confident that students have learned the vocabulary, move on to the first activity. Ask for student volunteers to read the five sentences aloud, or put students in pairs to take turns reading the sentences to each other. Finally, ask students to write out the sentences. If you have a set of the symbol cards, place the symbol for each word in the first sentence on the board and call on a student to come to the board and write out the sentence so that the rest of the class can check their work, or write out the answer on the board yourself.

Activity 2, Day 2: Paired Communicative Practice

1.

_____

2.

_____

3.

_____

4.

_____

5.

_____

Using the symbol cards, review the vocabulary from the day before. Make new sentences on the board, for example, *Thomas ist in der Küche* and ask for student volunteers to "read" the sentences. If you do not have a set of the symbol cards, ask students to say original sentences while referring to the symbols for Activity 1 in their books. Once you feel comfortable that students have retained yesterday's lesson, move on to the new vocabulary for Activity 2.

Introduce the symbol (on the board or in the book) for "where" and ask students to pronounce it after you. Place a symbol card for the bathroom on the board and ask where one of the characters is, for example, *Wo ist Brigitte?* Students should respond in a complete sentence: *Brigitte ist in dem Badezimmer.* Continue making sentences with other characters and the vocabulary for the other rooms of the house learned yesterday. Then introduce another neuter noun, the living room and another feminine noun, the garage, for today. Form sentences on the board using new and review vocabulary. If you do not have a set of the symbol cards, use Transparency 12 to practice the vocabulary. Point to a room in the house, for example, the dining room, and ask where one of the Symtalk characters is. Students should respond with the name of the room you are pointing to, for example, *Daniel ist in dem Esszimmer* or *Anton ist in der Garage.* Encourage students to get in the habit of responding in complete sentences from the very beginning.

Now students will be ready to learn the preposition "with." Review the sentences from yesterday's activity, and direct students to add "with" plus another character's name, for example, *Thomas ist in der Küche mit Silvia.* After sufficient practice with the preposition "with," ask for a student volunteer to come to the front of the classroom and engage in a short conversation with you:

Teacher:	*Wo ist Anton?*
Student:	*Anton ist in dem Wohnzimmer.*
Teacher:	*Anton ist in dem Wohnzimmer mit Hiko?*
Student:	*Nein, Anton ist in dem Wohnzimmer mit Brigitte.*

By using the prepositions and conjunctions in the Symtalk symbol cards set, students can create longer and longer sentences. Once you feel that students can produce the new vocabulary orally, write the new words on the board in the target language and ask students to copy them into their books.

Next, put students in pairs to ask and answer questions, as directed by the symbols in Activity 2. You may then want them to switch roles so each student has practice asking and answering the questions. Circulate around the room and help students converse naturally. Finally, ask students to write out the dialogues in their books.

Symtalk Symbol Cards Used in Exploring German

Note: When using the Symtalk Symbol Cards, be aware that there may be certain changes that take place when forming sentences. Examples:

der Kuchen
Er isst den Kuchen.

Sie zeichnet das Fahrrad.
Sie fährt mit dem Fahrrad.

Unit 1: Begrüßungen und Höflichkeit

1. Hallo! / *Hello!*

2. Wie geht's? / *How are you?*

3. Sehr gut. / *Very well.*

4. Danke. / *Thank you.*

5. Auf Wiedersehen! / *Good-bye.*

6. Bitte schön. / *You're welcome.*

7. Bis später! / *See you later!*

Unit 2: Die Klasse und Imperative

1. der Lehrer / *the teacher*

2. die Lehrerin / *the teacher*

3. sagt / *says*

4. Mach das Buch auf! Macht das Buch auf! / *Open your book.*

5. Setz dich! Setzt euch! / *Sit down.*

6. Hör zu! Hört zu! / *Listen.*

7. Geh! Geht! / *Go.*

8. an die Tafel / *to the board*

9. und / *and*

Unit 3: Die Zahlen

1. kostet, kosten / *costs, cost*

2. die CD / *the CD*

3. das Heft / *the notebook*

4. die Süßigkeiten / *the sweets*

5. die Karte / *the ticket*

6. die Sonnenbrille / *the sunglasses*

7. wie viel / *how much*

Unit 4: Die Geografie

1. wohnt, wohnen / *lives, live*

2. Paris / *Paris*

3. Wien / *Wien*

4. San Francisco / *San Francisco*

5. wo / *Where?*

Unit 5: Das Haus

1. ist / *is*

2. in dem, in der / *in the*

3. Schafzimmer / *bedroom*

4. Küche / *kitchen*

5. Badezimmer / *bathroom*

6. mit / *with*

7. Wohnzimmer / *living room*

8. Esszimmer / *dining room*

Unit 6: Die Familie

1. die Mutter / *the mother*

2. der Vater / *the father*

3. die Schwester / *the sister*

4. der Bruder / *the brother*

5. der Hund / *the dog*

6. wer / *who*

Unit 7: Die Tiere

1. was / *what*

2. die Kuh / *the cow*

3. das Schwein / *the pig*

4. mag / *likes*

5. die Vögel / *the birds*

6. die Katze / *the cat*

Unit 8: Die Berufe

1. ein Lehrer, eine Lehrerin / *a teacher*

2. ein Arzt, eine Ärztin / *a doctor*

3. ein Rechtsanwalt, eine Rechtsanwältin / *a lawyer*

4. ein Zahnarzt, eine Zahnärztin / *a dentist*

5. arbeitet / *works*

6. in dem Krankenhaus / *in the hospital*

7. in dem Büro / *in the office*

8. in der Schule / *in the school*

Unit 9: Das Essen

1. isst / *eats*

2. der Apfel / *the apple*

3. die Bananen / *the bananas*

4. der Kuchen / *the cake*

5. das Eis / *the ice cream*

6. der Käse / *the cheese*

Unit 10: Die Kunst

1. zeichnet / *draws*

2. ein Auto / *a car*

3. einen Park / *a park*

4. ein Haus / *a house*

5. ein Boot / *a boat*

6. ein Fahrrad / *a bike*

7. ein Strand / *a beach*

8. ein Geschenk / *a present, gift*

Unit 11: Der Körper und die Gesundheit

1. glücklich / *happy*

2. traurig / *sad*

3. krank / *sick*

4. müde / *tired*

5. böse / *angry*

6. wie / *how*

7. er (sie) / *he (she)*

Unit 12: Die Kleidung

1. trägt / *wears*

2. Schuhe / *shoes*

3. ein Hemd / *a shirt*

4. eine Hose / *pants*

5. eine Jacke / *a jacket*

6. ein Kleid / *a dress*

7. ein Hut / *a hat*

8. eine Kappe / *a cap*

9. Tennisschuhe / *tennis shoes*

10. Shorts / *shorts*

11. ein Rock / *a skirt*

Unit 13: Die Zeit und die Farben*

1. rot / *red*

2. rosa / *pink*

3. gelb / *yellow*

4. blau / *blue*

5. grün / *green*

*Although the colors appear here in grayscale, the symbol cards are solid squares of color.

Unit 14: Die Musik

1. hört, hören / *listens to, listen to*

2. die Musik / *the music*

3. CDs / *CDs*

4. Radio / *radio*

Unit 15: Das Wetter und die Jahreszeiten

1. Es ist schön. / *It's nice out.*

2. Es ist kalt. / *It's cold out.*

3. Es ist heiß. / *It's hot out.*

4. Es regnet. / *It's raining.*

5. Es schneit. / *It's snowing.*

Unit 16: Die Tage und die Monate

1. der Montag / *Monday*

2. der Dienstag / *Tuesday*

3. der Mittwoch / *Wednesday*

4. der Donnerstag / *Thursday*

5. der Freitag / *Friday*

6. der Samstag (Sonnabend) / *Saturday*

7. der Sonntag / *Sunday*

8. wann / *When*

Unit 17: Die Literatur

1. liest, lesen / *reads, read*

2. ein Buch / *a book*

3. ein Comic / *a comic*

4. eine Zeitung / *a newspaper*

5. eine Zeitschrift / *a magazine*

Unit 18: Die Freizeit

1. schwimmt , schwimmen / *swims, swim*

2. spielt, spielen / *plays, play*

3. Fußball / *soccer*

4. Baseball / *baseball*

5. Basketball / *basketball*

6. Volleyball / *volleyball*

Unit 19: Das Einkaufen

1. kauft, kaufen / *buys, buy*

2. ein Bleistift / *a pencil*

Unit 20: Das Reisen und der Verkehr

1. geht, gehen; fährt, fahren / *goes, go; ride*

2. mit dem Rad / *by bike*

3. zu Fuß / *on foot*

4. mit dem Bus / *by bus*

Using the Symtalk Symbol Cards

How to Introduce the Vocabulary

1. Point to the symbol cards and ask students to repeat several vocabulary words at a time. Ask questions in English to make sure they understand the meaning of each symbol.

2. Ask students to repeat the word or expression that goes with each symbol several times.

3. Combine the new vocabulary words in different ways to make phrases and sentences. Ask students to "read" the word groups.

4. Ask students to repeat parts of each symbol sentence as it develops.

5. Practice choral and individual repetition of the sentences.

6. Remove random cards from the sentences, replace them with question marks and encourage students to recall the missing symbol cards as they "read" the sentences again.

7. The Symtalk activities in Units 9, 10, 12, and 19 require the use of masculine accusative articles. Be sure to model the use of **den** and **einen** so that students can create sentences by themselves.

Activities Using the Symbol Cards

1. To review verb conjugations, place singular and plural character cards on the left of the board vertically, for example:

   Silvia
   Thomas und Anton

   Place a verb card, such as "to listen" to the right of the first character, for example, *Silvia*. Slide the verb card down so that students use the singular and plural form of the verb, for example, *Silvia hört* BUT *Thomas und Anton hören.*

2. Place a word bank on the board, made up of symbol cards (characters, nouns, verbs, conjunctions, etc.) that students have learned and that are placed in random order. Divide the class into two teams. Have the first player in Team A come to the board and make a sentence using the symbol cards. Have a student record the sentence so that there won't be any repeats. Then it's time for the first player from Team B, whose goal is to form a sentence that is different from the first sentence. Each sentence that is grammatically correct and logical wins a point for that team. The team with the higher number of points at the end of the allotted playing time is the winner.

3. Instruct students to pick a symbol sentence in their books. Ask them to write out the sentence on a piece of paper and hand it in. A student selects one of the papers turned in by the class and reads it aloud. Another student forms the sentence on the board using the symbol cards. The class compares the sentence on the board to the one in the book. Do any changes need to be made? Work as a class to correct the sentence.

4. Divide the class into two teams to play a version of baseball. Begin by placing the symbol cards for a sentence on the board in the target language, the longer the better, for example, *Silvia ist in dem Wohnzimmer mit Anton.* Then draw two baseball diamonds on the board, one for Team A and the other for Team B. The first student on Team A goes to the board and reads the original sentence aloud; then he or she changes one of the symbol cards to make a new, original sentence, for example, *Silvia ist in dem Esszimmer mit Anton.* If the student completes both tasks correctly, he or she advances to first base, designated by marking a stick figure along the side of the base with the student's initials. Now it is time for a player from Team B to take a turn. A run is scored after a team gets four correct sentences, thus arriving at home plate. The team having more runs wins. It is up to the instructor to decide when he or she should create a new sentence on the board for students to alter; it is a good idea to make a list of sentences ahead of time.

5. When you point to a symbol card, have students write down in the target language what the symbol card means. Or, ask students to use the word or expression in a new, original sentence.

General Tips for Using the Symbol Cards

1. Assess student retention of the meanings of the symbol cards frequently, perhaps as a daily warm-up activity.

2. Arrange all symbol sentences in a straight line.

3. Instruct from both the left and right side of the board.

4. Cover up the symbol cards so that students rely on their memory to reconstruct a sentence.

5. Call on students individually.

6. Provide plenty of choral practice.

7. Change the symbol cards frequently to keep up the momentum.

8. Repeat yourself often, adding and substituting different symbol cards.

9. Speak in the target language as much as possible when giving students direction.

10. Encourage creative self-expression in your students.

Note: When there are parentheses around a character in an activity, the pronoun should be used, for example, *die Mutter* becomes *sie* and *Thomas* becomes *er*.

Additional Information

Alphabet and Pronunciation Guide

Letter	German Pronunciation	Approximate Sound in English	Example
A	ah	ah	Apfel
B	beh	bay	Buch
C	tseh	say	Computer
D	deh	day	Datum
E	eh	ay	Essen
F	eff	eff	Familie
G	geh	gay	Garten
H	hah	hah	Heft
I	ih	ee	ich
J	jott	yott	Junge
K	kah	kah	kalt
L	ell	ell	Lampe
M	emm	emm	Mund
N	en	enn	Nase
O	oh	oh	Obst
P	peh	pay	packen
Q	kuh	koo	Qualität
R	err	air	reisen

S	ess	z—at beginning s—at middle/end	Sohn los
T	the	tay	Tag
U	uh	oo (as in "boot")	und
V	fau	fow	viel
W	weh	vay	Wagen
X	iks	iks	Xylofon
Y	üpsilon	erpsilahn	Yoga
Z	tset	tset	zehn

Other Sounds in German

Letter or Dipthong	German Pronunciation	Approximate Sound in English	Example
Ä	äh	ay	Mädchen
Ö	öh	u (as in "hurry")	Vögel
Ü	üh	ue	fünf
AU	au	ow	Haus
EI	ei	eye	eins
EU	eu	oy	heute
ß	ss	ss	Straße
SP	sch + p	shp	spielen
ST	sch + t	sht	Stadt

Information for Countries

(where German is listed as the official language* or is one of several official languages**)

German Name of Country	Capital City	Currency
Deutschland *	Berlin	der Euro
Liechtenstein *	Vaduz	der Franken (Swiss franc)
Österreich *	Wien	der Euro
Die Schweiz **	Bern	der Franken (Swiss franc)
Luxemburg **	Luxemburg	der Euro

Additional Notes

Unit 2: Classroom Objects

A *Schwamm*, or sponge, is often used in many German classrooms for cleaning the board. In addition to the word *Trockentafel*, the English term *white board* is often used to refer to a dry-erase board.

Unit 4: Geography

The porcelain commonly referred to as Dresden china is properly called Meißen china. It is manufactured in the Dresden suburb of Meißen.

The United Nations has four world headquarters: Vienna, Geneva, Nairobi, and New York.

Unit 5: House

A *Wohnmobil* is about the same as an RV camper.

IMPORTANT: Some of the phrases in the Symtalk section such as *in der Küche, in dem Schlafzimmer* require the dative case. The teacher may want to be aware of the grammar change and prepare students accordingly. These and other expressions that require some grammatical changes appear in this unit and in some of the later units.

Unit 17: Literature

Faust's pact: The scientist, Faust, makes an agreement with the devil, Mephistopheles. In return for information and truth, Faust promises that after his death Mephistopheles could claim his soul. In other words, the devil would provide all kinds of information to the intellectually curious scientist, but in exchange, Faust would give up his faith and hope for religious salvation.

Nussknacker und Mausekönig: A little girl falls asleep under her Christmas tree. Her best present, a nutcracker in the shape of a toy soldier, comes to life and conquers the evil mouse king.

Unit 20: Travel and Transportation

In the Symtalk section, the teacher may want to point out the difference between *gehen* (to go, walk) and *fahren* (to go by car, bus, etc.). The students should also be made aware of the irregular forms of *fahren (er/sie fährt)*.

Textbook Answer Key

Unit 1

A. 1. Ja.   2. Entschuldigung!   3. Viel Glück!   4. Tag!   5. Nein.

B. 1. Claudia   4. Bettina   5. Ruth   6. Heike   9. Sabine

C. 1. Ja. Ich spreche deutsch. (Nein. Ich spreche nicht deutsch.)
2. Ich heiße . . . *(name)*.
3. Gut, danke. Nicht schlecht.

D. 1. Viel Glück!
2. Guten Morgen! (Guten Tag!, Tag!)
3. Ich spreche deutsch.
4. Angenehm. (Es freut mich., Guten Tag! Tag! Auf Wiedersehen!)
5. Ich spreche englisch.
6. Gute Nacht!
7. Auf Wiedersehen!

E. 1. Guten Tag!   2. Guten Abend!   3. Angenehm. (Es freut mich.)   4. Viel Glück!   5. deutsch /
englisch   6. Robert   7. Nein.   8. Ich heiße . . . *(name)*   9. Auf Wiedersehen!   10. nein

F. 1. Ich heiße Lukas.   2. Gut, danke. Und dir?   3. . . . ich spreche deutsch.

G. *Answers will vary.*

H. *Answers will vary.*

I. 1. G   2. D   3. F   4. A   5. C   6. I   7. H   8. E   9. B

J. *Answers will vary.*

K. 1. Hallo!   2. Wie geht's?   3. Sehr gut.   4. Danke.   5. Auf Wiedersehen!   6. Bitte schön.
7. Bis später!

L. 1. Hallo! Wie geht's?   2. Sehr gut. Danke.   3. Danke. Auf Wiedersehen!   4. Bitte schön. Bis
später!

M. 1. Hallo, Thomas! / Hallo! Wie geht's? / Sehr gut. Danke.   2. Danke. Bis später! / Bitte schön.
Auf Wiedersehen!   3. Auf Wiedersehen, Brigitte! / Bis später, Silvia!

Kreuzworträtsel

A. *Answers will vary.*

B. *Answers will vary.*

C. 1. ein Lineal   2. eine Tafel   3. ein Bücherschrank   4. eine Landkarte   5. ein Bleistift   6. ein Kuli   7. ein Schreibtisch   8. ein Heft   9. ein Filzstift   10. ein Fenster   11. ein Buch   12. ein Stuhl   13. eine Uhr   14. ein Computer   15. eine Fahne

D. 1. Was   2. ein   3. eine   4. ein

E. *Answers will vary.*

F. 1. Sprich   2. Sag   3. Hör   4. Schalte . . . aus   5. Mach . . . auf

G. 1. ein Blatt Papier   2. Sätze   3. Buch   4. Bild   5. Computer   6. Kuli (Bleistift)   7. Frage

H. 1. Geh an die Tafel!   2. Schalte den Computer aus! (Schalte den Computer an!)   3. Heb die Hand!   4. Schreib!   5. Lies!

I. 1. B   2. E   3. D   4. C   5. A

J. *Answers will vary.*

K. *Answers will vary.*

L. *Answers will vary.*

M. 1. C   2. E   3. A   4. F   5. B   6. D

N. 1. 45 minutes   2. three (English, Latin, and Greek)   3. after 12:55   4. four times   5. on Wednesday at 12:10   6. five minutes

O. 1. der Lehrer   2. die Lehrerin   3. sagt   4. Mach das Buch auf! / Macht die Bücher auf!   5. Setz dich! / Setzt euch!   6. Hör zu! / Hört zu!   7. Geh! / Geht!   8. an die Tafel   9. und

P. 1. Der Lehrer sagt Brigitte „Setz dich!"
   2. Der Lehrer sagt Anton „Geh an die Tafel!"
   3. Die Lehrerin sagt Hiko „Mach das Buch auf!"
   4. Die Lehrerin sagt Silvia und Brigitte „Hört zu!"

Q. 1. Die Lehrerin sagt „Setzt euch!"
   2. Die Lehrerin sagt „Macht die Bücher auf!"
   3. Der Lehrer sagt „Hört!"

Kreuzworträtsel

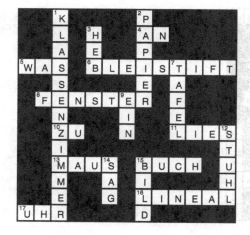

A. 1. eins 2. zwei 3. drei 4. vier 5. fünf 6. sechs 7. sieben 8. acht 9. neun 10. zehn

B. *Answers will vary.*

C. 1. 5 2. 8 3. 1 4. 9 5. 7

D. 1. drei 2. vier 3. sechs 4. zehn

E. 1. division 2. addition 3. multiplication 4. subtraction

F. 8 acht 3 drei 10 zehn 1 eins 9 neun 2 zwei 5 fünf 4 vier 7 sieben 6 sechs

G. 1. zwei 2. sechs 3. drei 4. eins 5. vier

H. 16, sechzehn

I. 1. achtundvierzig 2. zwanzig 3. zwei 4. dreißig 5. fünfzig 6. siebzig 7. fünfzehn
   8. vierzig 9. hundert 10. neunzehn

J. *Answers will vary.*

K. 1. square = vier 2. triangle = drei 3. hexagon = sechs 4. pentagon = fünf

L. 1. B 2. B 3. A 4. C 5. D

M. *Answers will vary.*

N. *Answers will vary.*

O. 1. zwanzig 2. sieben, Komma, acht 3. sechs, Komma, acht 4. dreiunddreißig
   5. vierundzwanzig 6. sechs, Komma, eins 7. zwei, Komma, drei 8. dreiundzwanzig
   9. siebzehn 10. neun, Komma, zwei

P. 1. null, acht, acht, zwei, eins, sieben, neun, sieben, neun, null, eins
   2. siebenundzwanzig
   3. acht, zwei, vier, sechs, sieben
   4. null, acht, acht, zwei, eins, sieben, neun, sieben, null

Q. 1. kostet, kosten 2. die CD 3. das Heft 4. die Süßigkeiten 5. die Karte
   6. die Sonnenbrille 7. wie viel

R. 1. Die Karte kostet acht Euro.
   2. Das Heft kostet sechs Euro.
   3. Die Süßigkeiten kosten neun Euro.
   4. Die Sonnenbrille kostet vierundzwanzig Euro.

S. 1. Wie viel kostet die CD? / Die CD kostet vierzehn Euro.
   2. Wie viel kostet das Heft? / Das Heft kostet fünf Euro.
   3. Wie viel kostet die Sonnenbrille? / Die Sonnenbrille kostet
      neunzehn Euro.
   4. Wie viel kostet die Karte? / Die Karte kostet zwanzig Euro.

Kreuzworträtsel

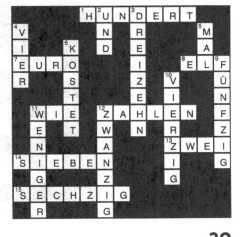

Unit 4

A. 1. G 2. I 3. F 4. K 5. J 6. D 7. H 8. C 9. E 10. A 11. L 12. B

B. 1. Wien 2. München 3. Köln 4. Leipzig 5. Berlin 6. Hamburg 7. Dresden
8. Salzburg 9. Zürich 10. Frankfurt 11. Bern 12. Frankfurt am Main

C. 1. Rhein (Rhine) 2. Donau (Danube) 3. Bodensee (Lake Constance) 4. Alpen (Alps)
5. Liechtenstein

D. 1. D 2. G 3. E 4. J 5. A 6. I 7. C 8. B 9. F 10. H

E. 1. Köln 2. Dresden 3. Wien 4. Berlin 5. Genf

F. 1. D 2. A 3. A 4. C 5. B 6. D 7. A 8. C 9. B 10. C

G. 1. North Sea 2. Baltic Sea 3. Austria 4. Denmark 5. Poland 6. The Czech Republic
7. Austria 8. Switzerland 9. France 10. Luxemburg 11. Belgium
12. The Netherlands 13. Gstaad 14. St. Moritz

H. *Answers will vary.*

I. *Answers will vary.*

J. *Places they'll visit:* Hameln, Passau, Würzburg, Göttingen, Landau / Isar, Kiel, Luzern, Potsdam
Their destination is: Potsdam

K. *Answers will vary.*

L. 1. nine 2. Dänemark 3. Nordsee 4. Ostsee 5. Kiel 6. east 7. Polen 8. Hannover
9. 70 10. Tschechische Republik 11. Wien 12. Mainz 13. 510 14. Brüssel 15.
Niederlande 16. Bern 17. Zürich 18. Braunschweig 19. kilometers (km)

M. 1. wohnt, wohnen 2. in Paris 3. in Wien
4. in San Francisco 5. wo

N. 1. Hiko wohnt in San Francisco.
2. Anton wohnt in Wien.
3. Daniel und Silvia wohnen in Paris.
4. Anton und Brigitte wohnen in Wien.

O. 1. Wo wohnt Brigitte? / Brigitte wohnt in Wien.
2. Wo wohnt Silvia? / Silvia wohnt in Paris.
3. Wo wohnt Hiko? / Hiko wohnt in San Francisco.
4. Wo wohnen Brigitte und Anton? / Brigitte und Anton wohnen in Wien.
5. Wo wohnen Silvia und Daniel? / Silvia und Daniel wohnen in Paris.

Kreuzworträtsel

Textbook Answer Key

Teacher's Guide

Unit 5

A. 1. das Wohnzimmer   2. das Schlafzimmer   3. das Badezimmer   4. das W.C.
    5. das Schlafzimmer   6. das Esszimmer   7. die Küche   8. das Schlafzimmer

B. 1. Küche   2. Schlafzimmer   3. Esszimmer   4. Badezimmer   5. Garten   6. Wohnzimmer /
    Terrasse

C. 1. dining room   2. kitchen   3. bedroom   4. bathroom   5. living room

D. 1. Esszimmer   2. Küche   3. Schlafzimmer   4. Wohnzimmer   5. Badezimmer   6. Küche
    7. Wohnzimmer   8. Esszimmer   9. WC / Badezimmer   10. Schlafzimmer

E. 1. das Zelt   2. die Wohnung   3. das Einfamilienhaus / die Eigentumswohnung   4. die Villa
    5. die Garage

F. 1. ZELT   2. ZIMMER   3. KÜCHE   4. HAUS   5. GARTEN

G. 1. B   2. C   3. C   4. A

H. *Answers will vary.*

I. *Answers will vary.*

J. *Answers will vary.*

K. 1. C   2. B   3. H   4. A   5. J   6. D   7. I

L. 1. Küche   2. Schlafzimmer   3. Wohnzimmer

M. 1. ist   2. in dem / in der   3. Schlafzimmer   4. Küche   5. Badezimmer   6. mit
    7. Wohnzimmer   8. Esszimmer

N. 1. Daniel ist in der Küche.
    2. Brigitte ist in dem Schlafzimmer.
    3. Silvia ist in der Küche.
    4. Thomas ist in dem Schlafzimmer.

O. 1. Wo ist Daniel? / Daniel ist in dem Badezimmer.
    2. Wo ist Anton? / Anton ist in dem Wohnzimmer mit Brigitte.
    3. Wo ist Silvia? / Silvia ist in dem Esszimmer mit Hiko.
    4. Wo ist Thomas? / Thomas ist in dem Schlafzimmer.
    5. Wo ist Brigitte? / Brigitte ist in dem Wohnzimmer mit Anton.

Kreuzworträtsel

Unit 6

A. 1. Schwester   2. Tochter   3. Enkelin   4. Schwester   5. Enkelin   6. Nichte   7. Tochter

B. 1. Mutter   2. Frau   3. Schwester   4. Tochter   5. Mann   6. Vater   7. Großvater

C. 1. ist meine Tante   2. ist mein Neffe   3. ist mein Großvater   4. ist meine Großmutter
   5. ist meine Kusine

D. 1. Bruder   2. Tante   3. Onkel   4. Großvater

E. 1. B   2. C   3. B

F. 1. Who's that?   2. Who am I?   3. Who is the man?   4. Who is speaking with Aunt Anneliese?

G. 1. Sohn   2. Tante   3. Bruder

H. I have a small family. My father is thirty-seven years old. My mother is thirty-eight years old. My sister's name is Tanja and she is nine. My brother's name is Dieter and he is six. My name is Alex and I'm thirteen. My family lives in Berlin. We have a house. My grandparents live in Leipzig. They have an apartment.

I. *Answers will vary.*

J. *Answers will vary.*

K. 1. D   2. B   3. H   4. A   5. B   6. E   7. F   8. A   9. C   10. G   11. D   12. F

L. *Answers will vary.*

M. 1. die Mutter   2. der Vater   3. die Schwester   4. der Bruder   5. der Hund   6. wer

N. 1. Die Mutter ist in dem Esszimmer.
   2. Der Bruder ist in dem Schlafzimmer.
   3. Die Schwester ist in dem Badezimmer.
   4. Der Vater ist in dem Wohnzimmer.

O. 1. Wer ist in der Küche? / Der Hund ist in der Küche.
   2. Wer ist in dem Schlafzimmer? / Silvia ist in dem Schlafzimmer.
   3. Wer ist in dem Wohnzimmer? / Der Vater ist in dem Wohnzimmer.
   4. Wer ist in dem Esszimmer? / Die Mutter ist in dem Esszimmer.
   5. Wer ist in dem Badezimmer? / Der Bruder ist in dem Badezimmer.

Kreuzworträtsel

Unit 7

A. 1. Ente   2. Kuh   3. Hund   4. Pferd   5. Vogel

B. *Some answers will vary.*

   1. Kuh (Pferd, Ziege)   2. Pferd (Kuh, Schwein, Ziege)   3. Ente   4. Vogel
   5. Katze (Hennen, Pferd, Kuh)

C. 1. C   2. B   3. A.   4. B   5. C   6. A

D. 1. D   2. C   3. E   4. A   5. B

E. 1. Vogel   2. Kaninchen   3. Ziege   4. Kuh

F. 1. Ein Esel ist groß.   2. Eine Katze ist klein.   3. Eine Ziege ist groß.   4. Ein Schwein ist groß.
   5. Ein Vogel ist klein.

G. 1. F   2. A   3. B   4. E   5. D   6. C

H. *Answers will vary.*

I. *Answers will vary.*

J. 1. A   2. D   3. C   4. B   5. C   6. A   7. D   8. C   9. B   10. D   11. A   12. D

K. 1. KATZE   2. SCHWEIN   3. PFERD   4. ENTE   5. VOGEL   6. KUH

L. 1. was   2. die Kuh   3. das Schwein   4. mag   5. die Vögel   6. die Katze

M. 1. Was sagt die Kuh? / Die Kuh sagt „muh."
   2. Was sagt der Hund? / Der Hund sagt „wau wau."
   3. Was sagt das Schwein? / Das Schwein sagt „grunz."

N. 1. Mag Daniel die Katzen? / Nein, Daniel mag die Hunde.
   2. Mag Brigitte die Hunde? / Nein, Brigitte mag die Katzen.
   3. Mag Hiko die Katzen? / Nein, Hiko mag die Vögel.
   4. Mag Anton die Vögel? / Nein, Anton mag die Kühe.
   5. Mag Silvia die Kühe? / Nein, Silvia mag die Schweine.

Kreuzworträtsel

Unit 8

A. *Answers will vary.*

B. 1. der Schauspieler, die Schauspielerin
2. der Landwirt, die Landwirtin
3. der Briefträger, die Briefträgerin
4. der Musiker, die Musikerin
5. der Programmierer, die Programmiererin; der Geschäftsmann, die Geschäftsfrau
6. der Krankenpfleger, die Krankenpflegerin; der Arzt, die Ärztin
7. der Koch, die Köchin
8. der Tischler, die Tischlerin
9. der Lehrer, die Lehrerin
10. der Mechaniker, die Mechanikerin

C. 1. LEHRER   2. LANDWIRT   3. ÄRZTIN   4. KÖCHIN   5. PROGRAMMIERER

D. 1. Beruf   2. bin   3. arbeite   4. du   5. Ich   6. machst   7. Briefträger (Briefträgerin)
8. gern

E. 1. My mother is a teacher.   2. She teaches in a school.   3. My father is a musician.
4. He plays the flute.   5. My cousin is a programmer.   6. She works with a computer.
7. My cousin is a cook.   8. He works in a restaurant.

F. 1. Programmierer   2. Ärztin   3. Elektriker   4. Tischlerin   5. Künstler   6. Köchin
7. Geschäftsmann   8. Landwirtin   9. Briefträger   10. Musikerin

G. 1. Arzt (Ärztin)   2. Briefträger (Briefträgerin)   3. Programmierer (Programmiererin)
4. Künstler (Künstlerin)   5. Tischler (Tischlerin)

H. *Answers will vary.*

I. *Answers will vary.*

J. 1. four   2. Ludwigsburg   3. for two days   4. 01 62-9 64 65 27   5. 28   6. in Berlin
7. secretary   8. July   9. Automobilverkäufer   10. Dresden   11. www.pcarbeit-nebenjob.de
12. sechzehn

K. 1. a) 42   b) 36   2. Chemikantin   3. Pharmakant

L. 1. Investition in die Zukunft *(Investment in the Future)*   2. Gersthofen

M. 1. ein Lehrer, eine Lehrerin   2. ein Arzt, eine Ärztin   3. ein Rechtsanwalt, eine
Rechtsanwältin   4. ein Zahnarzt, eine Zahnärztin   5. arbeitet   6. das Krankenhaus
7. das Büro   8. die Schule

N. 1. Der Vater ist ein Arzt.   2. Die Mutter ist eine Lehrerin.
3. Die Schwester ist eine Rechtsanwältin.   4. Der Bruder ist
ein Arzt.

O. 1. Wo arbeitet ein Arzt? / Ein Arzt arbeitet in dem
Krankenhaus.
2. Wo arbeitet ein Zahnarzt? / Ein Zahnarzt arbeitet in dem
Büro.
3. Wo arbeitet ein Lehrer? / Ein Lehrer arbeitet in der Schule.
4. Wo arbeitet ein Rechtsanwalt? / Ein Rechtsanwalt arbeitet
in dem Büro.

Kreuzworträtsel

Unit 9

A. 1. die Tasse   2. das Messer   3. das Glas   4. die Serviette   5. die Vase   6. der Tisch
7. der Käse   8. die Kekse

B. 1. vegetables   2. strawberries   3. sandwich   4. honey and spices   5. bread

C. *Possible Answers:*
1. meat: das Hähnchen, der Schinken, die Wurst, Schweinebraten, Hühnerfrikassee
2. vegetables: der Spinat, die Kartoffeln, die Zwiebeln, die grünen Bohnen
3. dairy products: die Butter, der Käse, das Eis, die Milch
4. beverages: der Orangensaft, die Milch, die Zitronenlimonade, die Limonade, das Mineralwasser
5. fruits: die Banane, die Apfelsine, die Birne, die Ananas, der Apfel
6. desserts: der Pudding, das Eis, die Kekse, Erdbeertorte, Lebkuchen

D. *Answers will vary.*

E. *Answers will vary.*

F. *Answers will vary.*

G. *Answers will vary.*

H. *Answers will vary.*

I. *Answers will vary.*

J. 1. 1.49   2. 1 kg (kilogram)   3. 5.00 euros   4. 3 kg   5. Spain   6. 3.58 euros
7. more oranges *(1 kg Orangen, 1 Grapefruit)*   8. pears *(Birnen)*

K. 1. fresh   2. quality   3. price   4. liter   5. vitamins   6. content

L. 1. isst   2. der Apfel   3. die Bananen   4. der Kuchen   5. das Eis   6. der Käse

M. 1. Thomas isst den Apfel.   2. Silvia isst die Bananen.   3. Anton isst den Kuchen.
4. Brigitte isst das Eis.   5. Hiko isst den Käse.

N. 1. Was isst Thomas? / Thomas isst den Apfel.
2. Was isst Silvia? / Silvia isst die Bananen.
3. Was isst Anton? / Anton isst den Kuchen.
4. Was isst Brigitte? / Brigitte isst das Eis.
5. Was isst Hiko? / Hiko isst den Käse.

Kreuzworträtsel

Unit 10

A. 1. *Lone Tree* 2. *Saint Anthony* 3. *The Young Hare* 4. *The Large Blue Horses* 5. *Ships in the Harbor of Greifswald* 6. *Women on the Street*

B. 1. Kirchner 2. Dürer 3. Dietz 4. Friedrich 5. Marc 6. Dürer

C. 1. F 2. A 3. D 4. B 5. E 6. C

D. 1. Friedrich 2. Kirchner 3. sculptures 4. *The Bridge* 5. Richter

E. 1. C 2. B 3. A

F. 1. Friedrich 2. Kirchner 3. Dietz

G. 1. Dürer 2. Kirchner (Marc) 3. Friedrich 4. Richter 5. Votteler and Dürer

H. *Answers will vary.*

I. 1. Kirchner 2. Dürer 3. Richter

J. *Answers will vary.*

K. 22 21 17 18 13 22 19 15 18 13 17 20

L. 1. university 2. opening times (hours of operation) 3. street 4. botanical garden 5. special museum 6. historical

M. 1. zeichnet 2. ein Auto 3. ein Park 4. ein Haus 5. ein Boot 6. ein Rad 7. ein Strand 8. ein Geschenk

N. 1. Daniel zeichnet ein Auto.
   2. Brigitte zeichnet einen Vogel.
   3. Hiko zeichnet einen Arzt.
   4. Anton zeichnet einen Park.
   5. Thomas zeichnet ein Haus.

O. 1. Was zeichnet Silvia? / Silvia zeichnet ein Boot.
   2. Was zeichnet Anton? / Anton zeichnet ein Rad.
   3. Was zeichnet Brigitte? / Brigitte zeichnet einen Strand.
   4. Was zeichnet Thomas? / Thomas zeichnet ein Geschenk.

Kreuzworträtsel

Unit 11

A. 1. der Kopf 2. der Hals 3. die Schulter 4. die Brust 5. der Arm 6. der Ellenbogen
   7. der Bauch 8. die Hand 9. das Bein 10. das Knie 11. der Fuß

B. 1. die Stirn 2. das Auge 3. das Ohr 4. die Nase 5. der Mund 6. der Zahn, die Zähne
   7. die Lippe, die Lippen 8. das Kinn

C. 1. Augen 2. Mund 3. Ohr 4. Hand 5. Zähne 6. Fuß 7. Nase 8. Finger
   9. Ellenbogen 10. Bauch

D. 1. speak 2. touch 3. see 4. hear 5. smell

E. 1. schlecht 2. wohl 3. krank 4. glücklich

F. 1. die Augen 2. die Nase 3. die Zähne 4. der Kopf 5. die Hand 6. das Haar
   7. der Hals 8. der Mund 9. die Ohren 10. der Finger

G. 1. H 2. A 3. E 4. B 5. D 6. G 7. J 8. C 9. F 10. I

H. 1. A 2. D 3. C 4. A 5. B

I. *Answers will vary.*

J. *Answers will vary.*

K. 1. two 2. She is a dentist. 3. I would go to Dr. Pohle. 4. 2197 5. Dr. Schröder
   6. Dr. Marszalek 7. Bahnhofstraße 40 8. Dr. Rechenauer

L. *Answers will vary.*

M. 1. glücklich 2. traurig 3. krank 4. müde 5. böse 6. wie 7. er / sie

N. 1. Brigitte ist krank. 2. Thomas ist müde. 3. Hiko ist traurig. 4. Siliva ist glücklich.
   5. Anton ist böse.

O. 1. Wie ist der Vater? / Er ist glücklich.
   2. Wie ist die Mutter? / Sie ist müde.
   3. Wie ist die Schwester? / Sie ist glücklich.
   4. Wie ist der Bruder? / Er ist krank.

Kreuzworträtsel

Unit 12

A. 1. E 2. F 3. G 4. D 5. I 6. A 7. J 8. C 9. H 10. B 11. L 12. K

B. *Possible Answers:*
1. Hose, Hemd, Rock, Bluse 2. Kleid, Anzug 3. Schlafanzug 4. Jacke, Pulli
5. Mantel, Hut, Handschuhe

C. 1. Hemd 2. Kleid (Anzug) 3. Schuhe 4. Bluse

D. 1. Kleid 2. Anzug 3. Bademantel 4. Rock, Bluse 5. Hemd, Krawatte

E. 1. to wear 2. he / she is wearing (has on) 3. I'm wearing (have on)
4. you are wearing (have on)

F. *outdoor clothing:* 1. Mantel 2. Jacke 3. Handschuhe 4. Hut
accessories: 5. Gürtel 6. Taschentuch 7. Krawatte
footwear: 8. Schuhe 9. Socken 10. Freizeitschuhe
sleepwear: 11. Schlafanzug

G. 1. A 2. D 3. A 4. B 5. C 6. D

H. 1. D 2. D 3. C 4. A

I. *Possible Answers:* Handschuhe, Hut, Mantel

J. *Answers will vary.*

K. *Answers will vary.*

L. 1. *sieben* 2. *Polyester* 3. 5.97 euros 4. No, also for ladies *(Damen)* 5. three pieces: *Jacke, Hose, Weste* 6. five 7. *Größen* 8. 1.99 euros, S–XXL (small through extra extra large)
9. in sizes 40–45 10. *Farbe (Farben)*

M. *Answers will vary.*

N. 1. trägt 2. Schuhe 3. ein Hemd 4. eine Hose 5. eine Jacke 6. ein Kleid 7. ein Hut
8. eine Kappe 9. Tennisschuhe 10. Shorts 11. ein Rock

O. 1. Thomas trägt ein Hemd. 2. Brigitte trägt eine Jacke. 3. Silvia trägt eine Hose.
4. Hiko trägt ein Kleid.

P. 1. Trägt Thomas eine Hose? / Nein, er trägt Shorts.
2. Trägt Anton eine Kappe? / Nein, er trägt einen Hut.
3. Trägt Brigitte ein Kleid? / Nein, sie trägt einen Rock.
4. Trägt Hiko Schuhe? / Nein, sie trägt Tennisschuhe.

Kreuzworträtsel

A. *Answers will vary.*

B. 1. rosa 2. blau 3. braun 4. gelb 5. grün 6. schwarz 7. orange 8. grau 9. weiß
10. rot

C. 1. Um sieben Uhr . . . 2. Es ist halb zwei. 3. Um zehn Minuten nach acht . . .
4. Es ist zwanzig Minuten vor drei. 5. Um zwanzig nach drei . . .

D. 1. D 2. E 3. A 4. B 5. C

E. 1. ja 2. nein 3. nein 4. nein 5. ja

F. 1. C 2. C 3. B 4. A 5. A 6. C

G. 1. nose: yellow 2. eyes: blue 3. hair: green 4. face: orange 5. mouth: brown
6. shoes: gray 7. 4: black 8. 6: purple 9. 3: red 10. E: white 11. i: pink 12. U: black

H. *Answers will vary.*

I. *Answers will vary.*

J. *Answers will vary.*

K. 1. im NDR um sechs (achtzehn Uhr)
2. im ZDF um Viertel nach vier (sechzehn Uhr fünfzehn)
3. im NDR um Viertel nach zwölf
4. im ZDF um fünf nach neun
5. im ARD um ein Uhr (dreizehn Uhr)
6. im ARD um fünf Uhr (siebzehn Uhr) und um fünf Uhr siebenundvierzig (17 Uhr
siebenundvierzig)
7. im ZDF um fünf (siebzehn Uhr)
8. im NDR um sechs Uhr fünfzig

L. 1. blau, gelb, rot, weiß 2. blau, gelb 3. rot, weiß 4. gelb, schwarz, rot, weiß
5. weiß, blau, gelb, rot 6. blau, weiß, rot, gelb

M. 1. rot 2. rosa 3. gelb 4. blau 5. grün

N. 1. Die Schuhe sind grün. 2. Die Kappe ist rot. 3. Das Hemd ist rosa.
4. Das Kleid ist grün. 5. Die Hose ist blau.

O. 1. Sind die Schuhe rot? / Nein, die Schuhe sind grün.
2. Ist die Hose grün? / Nein, die Hose ist blau.
3. Ist die Kappe blau? / Nein, die Kappe ist rot.
4. Ist das Hemd gelb? / Nein, das Hemd ist rosa.

Kreuzworträtsel

Unit 14

A. 1. Wolfgang Amadeus Mozart 2. Johann Sebastian Bach 3. Ludwig van Beethoven

B. 1. C 2. D 3. A 4. E 5. B

C. 1. Mozart 2. Bach 3. Beethoven 4. Beethoven 5. Bach

D. 1. Johann Sebastian 2. Bach 3. *Fidelio* 4. Salzburg 5. Mozart

E. 1. B 2. C 3. A

F. 1. Beethoven (*The Pastoral Symphony*) 2. Bach (St. Thomas Church) 3. Mozart (*The Magic Flute*)

G. *Answers will vary.*

H. *Answers will vary.*

I. 1. E 2. B 3. G 4. A 5. H 6. D 7. F 8. C

J. 1. 3 euros 2. 53111 3. on Sundays (or holidays) 4. I can send an email. 5. adults
   6. eight hours (10 A.M. to 6 P.M.)

K. 1. hört, hören 2. Musik 3. CDs 4. Radio

L. 1. Der Vater hört CDs. 2. Silvia hört Musik. 3. Anton hört Radio.
   4. Die Schwester und der Bruder hören CDs. 5. Brigitte hört Radio.

M. 1. Was hört Daniel? / Er hört Radio.
   2. Was hört Brigitte? / Sie hört Musik.
   3. Was hören der Vater und die Mutter? / Sie hören CDs.
   4. Was hört die Schwester? / Sie hört Radio.

Kreuzworträtsel

Unit 15

A. 1. E 2. D 3. A 4. C 5. B

B. 1. Es regnet. 2. Es ist wolkig. 3. Es ist windig. 4. Es schneit. 5. Es ist heiß.

C. 1. A 2. D 3. B 4. C

D. 1. sun / Sonne 2. lightning / Blitz 3. spring / Frühling 4. summer / Sommer
    5. weather / Wetter 6. autumn (fall) / Herbst 7. season / Jahreszeit 8. cool / kühl
    9. hot / heiß 10. It's raining. / Es regnet. 11. winter / Winter 12. bad / schlecht
    13. thunder / Donner 14. cold / kalt

E. 1. E 2. D 3. B 4. C 5. A

F. 1. Es ist kalt. 2. Es ist sonnig. 3. Es blitzt. 4. Es ist kühl. 5. Es ist schön.
    6. Es regnet. 7. Es schneit. 8. Es ist heiß. 9. Es ist windig. 10. Es ist schlecht.

G. 1. C 2. A 3. D 4. B

H. *Answers will vary.*

I. *Answers will vary.*

J. 1. Es regnet und es blitzt. 2. Es regnet und die Sonne scheint. 3. Die Sonne scheint.
    4. Es regnet und es blitzt. 5. Es regnet. 6. Es regnet und die Sonne scheint.

K. 1. siebzehn und fünf Grad 2. zwanzig Grad 3. vierzehn und vier Grad
    4. achtzehn und sechs Grad 5. sechzehn Grad 6. achtzehn und fünf Grad

L. 1. London 2. Berlin 3. Rom 4. Paris 5. Madrid 6. Warschau 7. Stockholm
    8. Athen

M. 1. Es ist schön. 2. Es ist kalt. 3. Es ist heiß. 4. Es regnet. 5. Es schneit.

N. 1. Es ist schön. 2. Es ist kalt. 3. Es regnet. 4. Es ist heiß. 5. Es schneit.

O. 1. Ist es heiß? / Nein, es ist kalt.
    2. Regnet es? / Nein, es ist schön.
    3. Schneit es? / Ja, es schneit.
    4. Ist es kalt? / Nein, es ist heiß.
    5. Regnet es? / Nein, es schneit.

Kreuzworträtsel

Unit 16

A. *Answers will vary.*

B. *Answers will vary.*

C. 1. Mittwoch, der 22. Oktober   2. Sonntag, der 13. August   3. Donnerstag, der 1. Mai
   4. Freitag, der 26. April   5. Samstag, der 9. Februar

D. 1. month: March; day: 5
   2. thunder
   3. mother: Freya (Freia); father: Odin (Wodan); son: Thor (Donner)

E. 1. B   2. C   3. C   4. A   5. B   6. A

F. 1. C   2. A   3. E   4. D   5. B

G. 1. März   2. Donnerstag   3. Freitag   4. April   5. Montag   6. Oktober   7. Februar
   8. *Answer will vary.*

H. 1. Sonntag   2. Donnerstag   3. Freitag   4. Samstag / Sonnabend   5. Montag
   6. Dienstag   7. Mittwoch

I. 1. A   2. B   3. D   4. C   5. A

J. *Answers will vary.*

K. *Answers will vary.*

L. 1. Am Sonntag.   2. Am Samstag und am Montag.   3. Am Samstag (Sonnabend).
   4. Am Samstag.   5. Am Freitag.   6. Am Mittwoch.   7. Am Donnerstag.   8. Am Dienstag.

M. 1. In November   2. At 8 P.M.   3. Tuesday through Friday   4. *Die Götterdämmerung*, 5 hours
   and 40 minutes

N. 1. Montag   2. Dienstag   3. Mittwoch   4. Donnerstag   5. Freitag
   6. Samstag, Sonnabend   7. Sonntag   8. wann

O. 1. Am Montag ist es schön.   2. Am Dienstag ist es kalt.   3. Am Mittwoch regnet es.
   4. Am Samstag ist es heiß.

P. 1. Wann trägt die Mutter das Kleid? / Am Montag trägt
      sie das Kleid.
   2. Wann trägt Daniel die Kappe? / Am Dienstag trägt er
      die Kappe.
   3. Wann trägt die Schwester das Kleid? / Am Freitag trägt
      sie das Kleid.
   4. Wann trägt Silvia die Hose? / Am Donnerstag trägt sie
      die Hose.
   5. Wann trägt Anton die Schuhe? / Am Dienstag trägt er
      die Schuhe.

Kreuzworträtsel

Unit 17

A. 1. Hoffmann 2. Schiller 3. Kirsch 4. Lasker-Schüler 5. Goethe 6. Wolf

B. 1. C 2. E 3. A 4. B 5. D

C.

Author	Type of Musical Version	Composers
1. Hoffmann	opera	Offenbach
2. Schiller	song within a symphony	Beethoven
3. Hoffmann	ballet	Tchaikovsky
4. Faust	opera	Gounod, Berlioz

D. 1. B 2. C 3. A

E. 1. Classical 2. Romantic

F. 1. Goethe 2. Lasker-Schüler 3. Schiller 4. Kirsch 5. Wolf 6. Hoffmann

G. *Answers will vary.*

H. 1. In 1857. 2. In Cleveland, Milwaukee, and San Francisco. 3. In 1775. 4. In 1832.
  5. In 1787. 6. A military academy. 7. Erich Kästner 8. In Hamburg. 9. 50 10. Welt
  11. Ich esse gern. 12. Karin Gündisch 13. In the Land of Chocolate and Bananas 14. 2

I. 1. liest, lesen 2. ein Buch 3. ein Comic 4. eine Zeitung 5. eine Zeitschrift

J. 1. Silvia liest ein Comic.
  2. Thomas liest eine Zeitung.
  3. Anton und Brigitte lesen eine Zeitschrift.
  4. Daniel liest ein Buch.

K. 1. Anton liest eine Zeitschrift in dem Park.
  2. Silvia liest ein Comic in dem Flugzeug.
  3. Silvia liest eine Zeitung an dem Strand.
  4. Anton liest ein Buch in dem Schlafzimmer.

Kreuzworträtsel

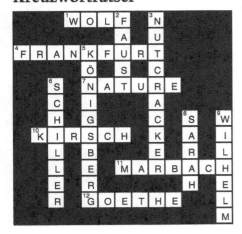

Unit 18

A. 1. Fußballspiel 2. Picknick 3. Party 4. Museum 5. Strand

B. 1. C 2. B 3. D 4. A 5. C

C. 1. Basketball 2. Fußball 3. Volleyball 4. Baseball 5. Tennis

D. 1. FREIZEIT 2. STRAND 3. MUSIK 4. PICKNICK 5. MUSEUM

E. 1. laufe 2. schwimme 3. lese 4. fahre 5. reite 6. tanze
   7. spiele amerikanischen Fußball

F. 1. du 2. Ich 3. los 4. findet 5. Party 6. Mädchen 7. gern

G. 1. A 2. C 3. A 4. D 5. B

H. *Answers will vary.*

I. *Answers will vary.*

J. 1. F 2. E 3. B 4. I 5. A 6. C 7. H 8. J 9. G 10. D

K. *Answers will vary.*

L. 1. schwimmt, schwimmen 2. spielt, spielen 3. Fußball 4. Baseball 5. Basketball
   6. Volleyball

M. 1. Daniel spielt Fußball.
   2. Silvia spielt Basketball.
   3. Anton und Brigitte spielen Volleyball.
   4. Die Mutter schwimmt.
   5. Der Bruder und die Schwester spielen Fußball.

N. 1. Spielt Brigitte Fußball? / Nein, sie spielt Volleyball.
   2. Spielt der Vater Volleyball? / Nein, er spielt Basketball.
   3. Schwimmt die Schwester? / Nein, sie spielt Fußball.
   4. Spielen Silvia und Daniel Basketball? / Nein, sie schwimmen.

Kreuzworträtsel

A. 1. B   2. A   3. E   4. C   5. D

B. 1. Pfirsiche   2. Markt   3. Einkaufszentrum   4. Kleingeld   5. kostet

C. 1. Geschäft   2. kaufen   3. Euro   4. billig   5. Kasse

D. 1. A   2. C   3. D   4. A   5. B

E. 1. I'm buying the tennis shoes.   2. You're buying seven peaches.   3. She's buying a CD.

F. 1. B   2. A   3. D   4. C   5. C

G. 1. sein   2. schaue   3. Angebot   4. kostet   5. teuer

H. *Answers will vary.*

I. *Answers will vary.*

J. 1. K   2. F   3. C   4. J   5. I   6. A   7. M   8. D   9. E   10. B   11. L   12. G   13. H

K. *Answers will vary.*

L. 1. kauft, kaufen   2. ein Bleistift

M. 1. Hiko kauft ein Kleid.
    2. Die Schwester kauft eine CD.
    3. Der Bruder kauft einen Bleistift.
    4. Silvia und Brigitte kaufen eine Karte.
    5. Anton und Daniel kaufen ein Heft.

N. 1. Wer kauft die Schuhe? / Daniel kauft die Schuhe.
    2. Wer kauft eine Kappe? / Anton kauft eine Kappe.
    3. Wer kauft eine Karte? / Die Mutter kauft eine Karte.
    4. Wer kauft ein Geschenk? / Der Vater kauft ein Geschenk.
    5. Wer kauft einen Bleistift? / Brigitte kauft einen Bleistift.

Kreuzworträtsel

A. 1. H 2. A 3. F 4. G 5. B 6. E 7. I 8. J 9. D 10. C

B. 1. mit dem Zug 2. mit dem Flugzeug 3. mit dem Schiff 4. mit dem Bus 5. mit dem Auto

C. 1. B 2. D 3. A 4. C 5. D

D. 1. FLUGSTEIG 2. KOFFER 3. FAHRPLAN 4. SCHALTER 5. BAHNHOF

E. 1. A 2. D 3. B 4. B 5. C

F. 1. reisen 2. Zug 3. Straße 4. Bahnsteig

G. *Answers will vary.*

H. *Answers will vary.*

I. 1. 25 km (kilometers) 2. south 3. 26,00 euros 4. B7 5. InterCityExpress
   6. Bad Berka 7. 4,50 euros 8. to the west 9. on the A71 10. Hermsdorfer Kreuz
   11. Frankfurt 12. 56 parking spots, open until 12 P.M.

J. 1. geht, gehen (fährt, fahren) 2. mit dem Rad 3. zu Fuß 4. mit dem Bus

K. 1. Daniel und Brigitte fahren mit dem Rad.
   2. Hiko geht zu Fuß.
   3. Anton und Silvia fahren mit dem Bus.
   4. Die Schwester fährt mit dem Rad.
   5. Der Vater fährt mit dem Bus.

L. 1. Brigitte geht zu Fuß mit einem Geschenk.
   2. Sie fährt mit dem Rad in den Park.
   3. Sie geht zu Fuß.
   4. Sie fährt mit dem Bus.

Kreuzworträtsel

Workbook Answer Key

Unit 1

A. 1. Claudia 2. Niklas 3. Petra 4. Heiko 5. Leonie 6. Andreas 7. Antje 8. Dieter
    9. Marie 10. Florian

B. *Mädchen:* Heike Elisabeth Johanna Beate Nele Gabriele
    Jungen: Simon Stefan Jochen Günther Eberhard Karsten

C. 1. D 2. C 3. F 4. B 5. A 6. E

D. 1. Florian 2. Ich 3. mich 4. Nein 5. Ja 6. russisch 7. danke 8. Bis
    9. Bitte schön. 10. heißt

E. 1. Germany, deutsch 2. Italy, italienisch 3. China, chinesisch 4. Russia, russisch
    5. Spain, spanisch 6. England, englisch 7. France, französisch 8. Japan, japanisch
    9. Egypt, arabisch

F. *Possible Names:* Antje, Leon
    Dialogue Answers: du; Antje; heiße Leon; freut; Angenehm.

G. *Answers will vary.*

H.

```
S E N E F P P N E G R O M S I B R
T H N V K B I C I X L Y X D T F V
G Z Y T F N B J Z A T O N K K W I
H L A B S T N U B P R E Q I P F M
I V I A Z C N T H B B Q M J O T L
S X X S A P H E R A T N Z A L I V
G G U B M K I U N X E L S Z J V J
U X Z W Z R Q E L M E H B R J J M
T Q S K A E T Y A D O N V L V W X
E U G M Z U F N S K I B I W M N X
N H D W G N H Y I M C G A K Q E F
T Q I H P I E V N E F P U F L U I
A M Y S L V A R C W S Q Q N P A H
G A O X I L D D A F C K K G G Q S
T I M A L L P T Z B I T T E Q N S
```

1. ENTSCHULDIGUNG   6. NIKLAS

2. MARIE   7. GUTENTAG

3. GUTENABEND   8. BISMORGEN

4. NAMEN   9. JA

5. BITTE

I. 1. *bitte*   2. last or family name   3. first name   4. adult   5. zip code   6. *Herzlich willkommen!*   7. in the morning   8. luck   9. that you are thankful / your gratitude   10. world

Unit 2

A. 1. D   2. A   3. C   4. B   5. E

B. 1. Wischer   2. Schreibtisch   3. Wand   4. Filzstift   5. Kuli   6. Bleistift   7. Buch   8. Stuhl   9. Computer   10. Tastatur

C. 1. eine Uhr   2. eine Landkarte   3. ein Buch   4. ein Papier (ein Blatt Papier)   5. ein Stuhl

D. *Possible Answers:*   1. ein Buch   2. ein Kuli   3. ein Bleistift   4. ein Heft   5. ein Lineal

E. 1. ein Buch   2. eine Landkarte   3. ein Stuhl   4. ein Schreibtisch   5. ein Kuli

F. 1. A   2. B   3. A   4. B   5. A   6. A

G. 1. Hand   2. deutsch   3. Tafel   4. Frage   5. Computer   6. Bild   7. Buch

H. 1. Schreib!   2. Lies!   3. Hör zu!   4. Mach das Fenster auf (zu)!   5. Schalte den Computer an (aus)!

I. *Answers will vary.*

J. *Answers will vary.*

K. 1. German   2. Druckschrift   3. ä, ö, ü, ß, Ä, Ö, Ü   4. after the letter "z" and "Z"   5. ß   6. 53,36 Euro (€)   7. 10   8. 6,90 Euro (€)

Unit 3

A. 1. B   2. C   3. A   4. A   5. C   6. B

B. 1. G   2. J   3. A   4. D   5. E   6. B   7. F   8. H   9. I   10. C

C. 1. neunzehn   2. vier   3. zehn   4. fünfzig   5. achtzig

D. 1. acht   2. zehn   3. vier   4. zweiundfünfzig   5. sechsundzwanzig   6. zwölf   7. dreißig   8. sechzig   9. einunddreißig   10. eins

E. 1. $30 - 20 = 10$ 2. $200 + 200 = 400$ 3. $13 \times 1 = 13$ 4. $20 \div 4 = 5$

F. 1. Drei mal vier ist zwölf.
   2. Sieben und fünfzehn ist zweiundzwanzig.
   3. Tausend weniger zweihundert ist achthundert.
   4. Sechzehn geteilt durch acht ist zwei.
   5. Dreißig und vierzig ist siebzig.
   6. Neun weniger fünf ist vier.
   7. Siebenundzwanzig geteilt durch drei ist neun.
   8. Vierzehn mal eins ist vierzehn.
   9. Zwölf und eins ist dreizehn.
   10. Fünfundsechzig weniger vier ist einundsechzig.

G. *Answers will vary.*

H. *Answers will vary.*

I. *Answers will vary.*

J. 1. sieben   2. fünfhundert   3. acht   4. drei   5. eins (ein Cent)   6. achtzig Cent

Unit 4

A. 1. C   2. B   3. D   4. E   5. A

B. 1. C   2. A   3. C   4. B   5. B

C. 1. die Donau   2. Zürich   3. der Rhein   4. Hamburg   5. Bern   6. Berlin   7. Salzburg
    8. Genf   9. der Main   10. Dresden   11. die Elbe   12. Wien   13. Leipzig
    14. Frankfurt am Main   15. München   16. Köln

D. *Answers will vary.*

E. 1. Lake Constance, located on Germany's southern borders with Austria and Switzerland
    2. North Sea, body of water in the northwest
    3. Baltic Sea, body of water in northeast
    4. Alps, a mountain range in southern Germany, Austria and Switzerland
    5. Harz Mountains, small mountain range in central Germany

F. 1. N   2. S   3. W   4. NW   5. NE   6. SW   7. SE   8. E

G. 1. der Main   2. der Rhein   3. die Elbe   4. die Donau   5. der Rhein

H.

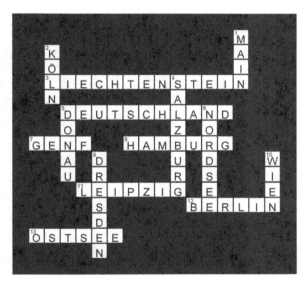

I. 1. *Österreich* (Austria)   2. hiking   3. summer   4. hotels for hiking guests   5. yes
    6. riding a cable car up a mountain   7. *Kärnten*   8. *Berge*

Unit 5

A. 1. C   2. D   3. E   4. F   5. G   6. A   7. B

B. 1. recliner   2. shower   3. refrigerator   4. bedspread   5. automotive tools   6. tablecloth

C. 1. Wo wohnst du?   2. Wie viele Schlafzimmer gibt es?   3. Wo ist die Küche ?
   4. Wie viele Badezimmer gibt es?

D. 1. *(name of city or town)*   2. Ja.   3. *(Answer will vary.)*   4. Ja   5. gibt   6. Blumen

E. 1. die Hütte   2. die Villa   3. die Terrasse   4. die Wohnung   5. das Mietshaus

F. *Answers will vary.*

G. *Answers will vary.*

H. *Sample Answers:*
   1. Frau Schmidt wohnt in Wien.
   2. Herr Weber wohnt in Zürich.
   3. Elisabeth wohnt in Dresden.
   4. Die Familie Meier wohnt in Hamburg.
   5. Klaus wohnt in Wien.

I. 1. happy   2. fresh ideas   3. lamps and lights   4. 1,95 €   5. *das Wohnzimmer*
   6. to decorate, Haus, atmosphere, magazine

Unit 6

A. 1. J   2. I   3. D   4. A   5. H   6. G   7. B   8. F   9. E   10. C

B. 1. A   2. C   3. A   4. B   5. A   6. C   7. C   8. B

C. *Answers will vary.*

D. *Answers will vary.*

E. *Answers will vary.*

F. *Answers will vary.*

G. 1. (your name)   2. *ja / nein*   3. (number of cousins)   4. (his name)   5. *ja / nein*

H.

I. 1. They are about children.   2. *Es gibt drei Briefmarken.*   3. the value of the stamp: *55 Cent*
4. protect children from traffic hazards   5. *Hier machen Familien gern Urlaub.*   6. *zwei*
7. telephone and fax numbers   8. *Österreich*

Unit 7

A. 1. Das ist eine Kuh.   2. Das ist eine Katze.   3. Das ist ein Vogel.   4. Das ist ein Pferd.

B. 1. Pferd   2. Schwein   3. Katze   4. Kaninchen   5. Hund   6. Vogel

C. das Pferd, das Schwein, der Hund, die Ente

D. *Sample Answers:*   1. Lande   2. Tiere   3. Pferd   4. helfen   5. Max

E. 1. Weide   2. Stall   3. Scheune   4. Teich   5. Luft

F. 1. Der Hund ist klein.   2. Die Katze ist klein.   3. Das Pferd ist groß.   4. Die Esel sind groß.
5. Die Hennen sind klein.

G. 1. B   2. A   3. B   4. A   5. B   6. B   7. A   8. B

H. *Answers will vary.*

I.

```
X K J W N O G V V I P T F S S B O
A P G L I Q S V G B A B M O F F S
P A K T S R M D N A L X X N I J R
F D R E F P Y V O R H V M B L N A
E I C O X M C N J X J Y L Q E E C
L J Y T H Y J G Y B H K J X S Z T
P J O E Y V M K G D R U C E E P C
U N S N E H C N I N A K N P K K A
N H B U V F L O Q L D E Y D P W I
N C T H E J O V Y M U Z A M Q V F
R I J T X N D Z J O U T P K F L A
Q E L U N Z U G W X E A I Z L T V
A T J S I X W E I D E K G A B E O
T A B Y N Z Y W H B B K T F W Y G
I J K C S L U F T C T S K N P G E
X N T M A D I P P E S E V U R Q L
L G J T E E N T E Y I H K Y H T P
```

1. ESEL	5. PFERD	9. KANINCHEN	13. KATZE
2. APFEL	6. VOGEL	10. ENTE	14. HUND
3. KUH	7. STALL	11. WEIDE	15. LUFT

J. 1. *Tierfreund* 2. A friend to animals (literally: an animal friend) 3. us 4. *Der Delphin ist groß.* 5. *drei* 6. *Perserkatzen* (Persian cats) 7. *Wellensittiche* 8. horses

Unit 8

A. 1. E 2. F 3. I 4. H 5. C 6. G 7. A 8. J 9. B 10. D

B. 1. A 2. C 3. B 4. C 5. A 6. C

C. 1. Arzt 2. Künstlerin 3. Tischler 4. Klempnerin 5. Elektriker 6. Köchin
   7. Programmierer 8. Schauspielerin 9. Geschäftsmann 10. Krankenpflegerin

D. 1. Was 2. Briefträger 3. machst 4. arbeite 5. Programmierin. 6. der
   7. Krankenpfleger 8. ist 9. Köchin 10. Arbeitsstelle

E. *Answers will vary.*

F. 1. Landwirt / Landwirtin
   2. Musiker / Musikerin
   3. Koch / Köchin
   4. Briefträger / Briefträgerin
   5. Schauspieler / Schauspielerin
   6. Krankenpfleger / Krankenpflegerin; Arzt / Ärztin
   7. Programmierer / Programmiererin; Geschäftsmann / Geschäftsfrau

G. *Answers will vary.*

H.

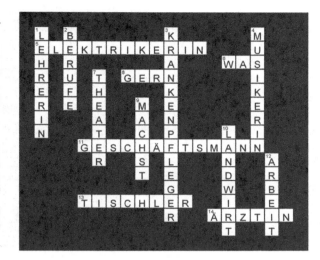

I. 1. *Moderne Berufe für junge Leute*   2. *Ausbildung*   3. workplace   4. repair and maintain
    agricultural machinery   5. *sechs*   6. veterinarian   7. *Kleintiere* (small animals)   8. Ulrike
    9. in Wallersdorf

Unit 9

A. 1. D   2. C   3. B   4. A   5. C

B. *Answers will vary.*

C. 1. F   2. I   3. C   4. A   5. H   6. B   7. G   8. E   9. J   10. D

D. 1. C   2. A   3. B   4. B   5. A   6. A   7. C   8. B   9. C   10. A

E.

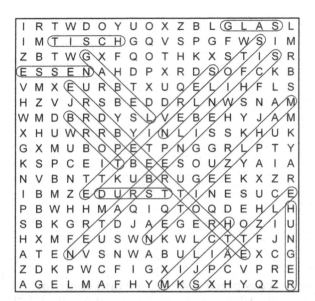

1. ESSEN	8. ERDBEERTORTE
2. STOLLEN	9. SPÄTZLE
3. SCHWEINEBRATEN	10. GLAS
4. MILCH	11. TISCH
5. SERVIETTE	12. GABEL
6. MAHLZEITEN	13. BROT
7. HUNGER	14. DURST

F. *Answers will vary.*

G. *Answers will vary.*

H. Answers will include: *Gut. Ich habe Hunger. Danke. Ein(en) Apfel, bitte*

I. 1. *Brot, Kuchen* 2. *Doppelback* 3. *-,89 Cent* 4. *Tomaten* 5. *Aprikosenkuchen,* apricot cake
   6. *Obst* 7. *für 12 Stücke* 8. *Vanilleis,* vanilla ice cream

Unit 10

A. 1. Kirchner or Marc 2. Dürer 3. Richter, Rauch and Weischer 4. Votteler 5. Dietz

B. 1. Friedrich 2. Rauch and Weischer 3. Kirchner and Marc 4. Dürer

C. 1. Kirchner 2. Dürer 3. Marc 4. Friedrich 5. Dietz 6. Votteler
   7. Richter, Weischer or Rauch

D. *Students should draw:* 1. a pen 2. a computer 3. a tent 4. a cabin 5. a dog 6. a fork
   7. a spoon 8. a knife

E. *Students should draw:* 1. a boy reading a book 2. a girl speaking with a male letter carrier
   3. a boy petting a cat 4. five plates on a table

F. 1. *Kunstwerke* 2. *Kunstobjekte* 3. the art of making books 4. the art of making clocks
   5. the art of making jewelry 6. the art of making lawn decorations

G.

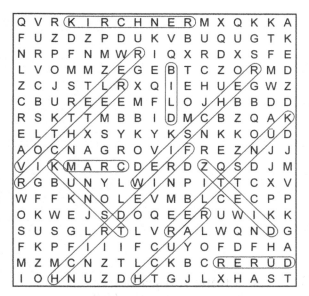

1. KUNST 4. KÜNSTLER 7. DIETZ 10. VOTTELER

2. RICHTER 5. RAUCH 8. WEISCHER 11. KIRCHNER

3. MARC 6. FRIEDRICH 9. DÜRER 12. BILD

H. *Answers will vary.*

Unit 11

A. 1. I 2. E 3. A 4. F 5. G 6. H 7. B 8. J 9. C 10. D

B. 1. B 2. B 3. A 4. A 5. A

C. 1. S 2. r 3. s 4. e 5. M 6. h 7. t 8. u 9. B 10. a

D. 1. die Nase 2. die Zähne 3. der Mund 4. der Arm 5. die Finger *(plural)*
    6. das Ohr (die Ohren) 7. das Auge 8. der Kopf

E. 1. Brust 2. Hals (Kopf) 3. Ellenbogen 4. Knie 5. Bauch 6. Nase 7. Stirn
    8. Gesicht 9. Finger 10. Zähne

F. *Positive:* Ich bin glücklich. die Gesundheit Es geht mir gut. gesund
    Negative: Ich bin traurig. Es geht mir schlecht. Kopfweh krank

G. 1. du, Kopfweh 2. hast, Grippe 3. geht 4. fühle 5. gesund

H. 1. Ich fühle mich wohl. 2. Ich fühle mich schlecht. 3. Ich bin glücklich.
    4. Ich bin traurig.

I. *Answers will vary.*

J. *Answers (Pictures) will vary.*

K.

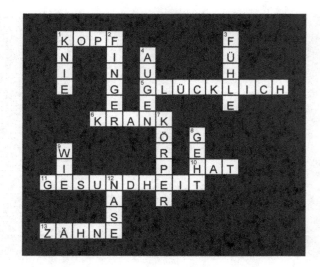

L. 1. *dicht* – heavy   2. *zu* – clogged, stuffed up   3. *ja*   4. I hope you get better.
    5. *der Wald, das Wasser*   6. *das Wasser*   7. *der Wald*   8. *Wir müssen draußen bleiben.*

Unit 12

A. 1. J   2. E   3. C   4. H   5. A   6. D   7. G   8. F   9. B   10. I

B. 1. C   2. B   3. C   4. A   5. C

C. 1. der Bademantel   2. die Handschuhe   3. das Taschentuch   4. der Gürtel
    5. der Hut, die Baseball-Mütze   6. die Schuhe

D. 1. Bluse   2. Anzug   3. Strickjacke   4. Schuhe   5. Socken

E. 1. die Socken   2. die Bluse   3. die Schuhe   4. das Hemd   5. der Hut   6. das Kleid

F.

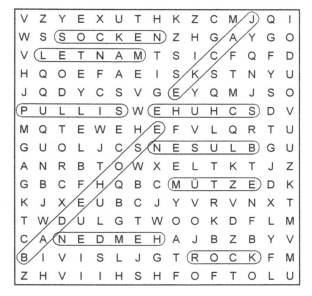

1. JACKE 4. MANTEL 7. ROCK 9. MÜTZE

2. PULLIS 5. SCHUHE 8. HEMDEN 10. BLUSEN

3. SOCKEN 6. BADEHOSE

G. *Answers will vary.*

H. 1. Anzug, Konzert 2. Jacke, Garten 3. Bademantel, Badezimmer 4. schön 5. klein

I. 1. *Montag, 27. März* (Monday, March 27) 2. *Stepp-Jacken* 3. sporty 4. light-weight
    5. *Innentasche , Handy-Tasche* 6. in a pocket *(Handy-Tasche)* 7. *Größen* 8. 9,99 €

Unit 13

A. 1. A 2. B 3. B 4. A 5. B

B. 1. 9:45 2. 3:30 3. 8:00 P.M. 4. 5:17 5. 1:00 6. 7:45 7. 11:50 8. 4:20
    9. 12:00 midnight 10. 12:00 noon

C. 1. 1:00 P.M. 2. 10: 00 P.M. 3. 5:40 P.M. 4. 11: 51 P.M. 5. 6:25 P.M.

D. 1. rot 2. grau 3. weiß 4. gelb 5. schwarz 6. blau 7. orange 8. braun 9. grün
    10. violett

E. 1. blau und gelb 2. rot und gelb 3. schwarz und weiß 4. rot und weiß 5. blau und rot

F.

G. *Answers will vary.*

H. *Answers will vary.*

I. 1. It shows two ways of telling time. 2. *Es ist halb zwei.* 3. quarter before / of
    4. one and one-half hours 5. *17 Uhr* 6. medium brown 7. dark blue 8. light yellow

Unit 14

A. 1. St. Matthew Passion 2. The Magic Flute 3. Brandenburg Concertos
    4. The Sixth Symphony (AThe Pastoral@) 5. Jupiter Symphony

B. 1. Bach 2. Mozart 3. Beethoven 4. Bach 5. Beethoven

C. 1. C 2. B 3. A 4. C 5. C 6. A 7. B 8. A 9. B 10. C

D. 1. LUDWIG 2. JOHANN 3. WOLFGANG 4. SEBASTIAN 5. AMADEUS

E. 1. B 2. E 3. F 4. A 5. C 6. D 7. G

F. D 2. C 3. B 4. F 5. E 6. A

G. *Answers will vary.*

H. 1. *Eintritt* 2. Bach 3. Eisenach 4. 4 euros 5. visitor number 6. in Brixen (German
name for Bressanone, Italy) 7. Luca Scandali 8. *Um 20.30.* (8:30 P.M.)

Unit 15

A. 1. D 2. J 3. H 4. G 5. F 6. A 7. E 8. B 9. I 10. C

B. 1. kalt 2. warm, heiß 3. kühl, windig 4. regnet 5. schneit 6. sonnig 7. Es blitzt.

C. 1. der Sommer   2. der Frühling   3. der Winter   4. der Herbst   5. der Sommer

D. 1. der Herbst   2. der Winter   3. der Sommer   4. der Frühling   5. der Herbst
6. der Frühling

E. 1. Es ist schön.   2. Es ist kalt.   3. Es ist warm.   4. Es schneit.   5. Es ist kühl.
6. Es ist schwühl.   7. Es blitzt.   8. Es donnert.

F. 1. Es ist sonnig und heiß.   2. Es ist kalt.   3. Es regnet.   4. Es blitzt.   5. Es schneit.
6. Es ist heiß.   7. Es ist kühl.   8. Es ist windig.   9. Es ist wolkig.   10. Es ist schwühl. /
Es ist heiß.   11. Es ist kalt.

G. *Answers will vary.*

H.

```
G Z D G Q Q M L Ü W H C S C F K
V H P O C L X Y C P Q V M J U C
G S O M M E R B L H Ü K Z B W L
N C B B Z D K F F G L L H X V R
I W O L K I G D H W E T T E R Z
L N Z K B L Z Y R W Q R C K W
H L B A L T H B V I M H E T K E
Ü X Z M N T D K C B W L B L S J
R O Q R U S I D I R L N M T U A
F S G T S B R E H R M T C L W H
O N I L C Z B Y W A R M K I Y
X F Z E N A L G C X Z A A G N K
T K L B Z N M H E A S L A F T R
N F Q S W M O Q X W T K R Q E U
I I B M X N B S F A L M Z X R N
R V X K W Y C U S K L H J T Q I
```

1. KÜHL   4. SONNIG   7. WARM   10. WETTER

2. WIND   5. WOLKIG   8. WINTER   11. HERBST

3. FRÜHLING   6. SOMMER   9. SCHWÜL   12. KALT

I. 1. showers   2. storms   3. *nein*   4. *nein*   5. 32°C (centigrade)   6. *nein*   7. *warm und sonnig*
8. *ja*

Unit 16

A. 1. E   2. H   3. B   4. J   5. D   6. A   7. C   8. I   9. G   10. F

B. 1. Montag   2. Dienstag   3. Mittwoch   4. Donnerstag   5. Freitag   6. Samstag
7. Sonntag

C. 1. Donnerstag   2. morgen   3. Januar   4. Samstag (Sonnabend)   5. September

D. 1. Samstag, der 6. Juni   2. Mittwoch, der 13. Oktober   3. Sonntag der 19. Dezember
4. Freitag, der 21. Mai   5. Dienstag, der 7. August

E. 1. der 1. April   2. der 4. Juli   3. Februar   4. Freitag   5. Dienstag   6. Oktober   7. Mai
8. Juni   9. Montag   10. Sonntag

F. 1. B   2. A   3. B   4. A   5. A

G. *Answers will vary.*

H. 1. Sonnabend   2. Januar   3. Geburtstag   4. Feiertag   5. Dezember   6. Wochenende

I. 1. no   2. as of June 8th   3. *Eislauf*   4. end of April to beginning of July   5. yes
6. on Mondays   7. 7:30–9:00 P.M.   8. on Thursdays

Unit 17

A. 1. Sarah Kirsch   2. Johann Wolfgang von Goethe   3. Friedrich Schiller   4. Christa Wolf
5. Else Lasker-Schüler   6. E.T.A. Hoffmann

B. 1. play   2. play   3. poetry   4. story   5. poetry

C. 1. E   2. A   3. B   4. C   5. D

D. 1. Sarah Kirsch   2. Johann Wolfgang von Goethe   3. Ernst Theodor Amadeus Hoffmann
4. Else Lasker-Schüler   5. Friedrich Schiller

E. 1. Berlin   2. Frankfurt   3. German Democratic Republic   4. German Democratic Republic
5. Königsberg   6. Marbach

F. *Answers will vary.*

G.

H. 1. books for girls and boys   2. 10–16 years   3. *die Bücher*   4. Cornelia Funke   5. *Die Wolke,*
by Gudrun Pausewang   6. Dietrich Grönemeyer   7. *22,50 Euro*   8. *Taschenbuch*

Unit 18

A. 1. D   2. H   3. I   4. G   5. A   6. B   7. E   8. J   9. C   10. F

B. 1. Ich gehe auf die Party.   2. Ich gehe zum Fußballspiel.   3. Ich gehe ins Museum.
    4. Ich gehe zum Strand.

C. 1. Baseball   2. Rad   3. los   4. klar   5. mitkommen   6. tanze

D. 1. C   2. A   3. B   4. B   5. A   6. C

E.

```
K P J S I W R O V T D V J L L K M
C V G J Y M C P F R Y V W A L O O
X F P A R A D F A H R E N B A P D
C D R C R G F O E R W X K A B H N
Z V H E Q Z J M W F T K X I Y G A
H I P C I Q D L I H N Y K L E V R
N P Q Z X Z N P E T H I L L L S T
E U N E T I E R D Y K A R O L B S
L U G K L A F I W K B O I B O O U
E N R T N C P C T S N J M Z V U F
I M R G E A V E S G F M B M A M O
P X M R S T S U T H Q Y L R E S T
S Z Z S E F F P I C K N I C K N D
Z J C P U I A U M U E S U M H M K
```

1. RADFAHREN   5. SPIELEN   9. VOLLEYBALL
2. FUSSBALL   6. MITKOMMEN   10. FREIZEIT
3. MUSEUM   7. STRAND   11. PARTY
4. PICKNICK   8. REITEN   12. LESEN

F. 1. Ich gehe heute Abend auf die Party.
    2. Ich gehe morgen zum Picknick.
    3. Ich gehe am Samstag ins Museum.
    4. Ich gehe am Sonntag zum Strand.

G. 1. Ich spiele Baseball.   2. Ich spiele Volleyball.   3. Ich spiele Tennis.
    4. Ich spiele Basketball.   5. Ich spiele Fußball.

H. *Answers will vary.*

I. 1. postage stamps   2. young and old   3. *Philatelie*   4. fun collecting things (in this case,
    stamps)   5. 10 *Cent*   6. *ja*   7. *Leuchttürme*   8. *Integration, Unsere Zukunft*

Unit 19

A. 1. B   2. C   3. A   4. C   5. A   6. B   7. A   8. A   9. B   10. B

B. 1. Pfirsiche   2. Wie viel   3. Auswahl   4. alles   5. Kleingeld

C. *Answers will vary.*

D. 1. C   2. A   3. C   4. B   5. A   6. A

E. 1. kaufen   2. Tomaten (Pfirsiche, CDs)   3. billig   4. Wohin   5. Ja

F. 1. Was darf es sein?
   2. Wie viel kostet dies CD?
   3. Sie kostet 29 Euro.
   4. Gut. Ich kaufe die CD. Hier ist das Geld.
   5. Danke schön. Noch etwas?
   6. Nein, das ist alles.

G. 1. grüne Bohnen   2. ein Bleistift   3. Pfirsiche   4. Tennisschuhe   5. ein Buch   6. eine CD
   7. ein Rad

H. *Answers will vary.*

I. 1. *Spitzentechnik*   2. *299,- Euro*   3. user-friendly   4. skim milk   5. *Liter*   6. *-,49 Cent*
   7. *Das ist ein Glas Milch.*   8. *Es gibt zwei Kühe.*

Unit 20

A. 1. B   2. C   3. A   4. B   5. C

B. 1. nächste   2. die   3. Park   4. komme   5. Flugsteig

C. 1. D   2. A   3. E   4. B   5. C

D. 1. Ich fliege. (Ich reise mit dem Flugzeug.)
   2. Ich reise (fahre) mit dem Zug.
   3. Ich reise (fahre) mit dem Schiff.
   4. Ich reise (fahre) mit dem Auto.
   5. Ich reise (fahre) mit dem Bus.

E. 1. Bahnhof   2. Frankfurt   3. Schalter   4. Fahrkarte   5. Zug

F. *Answers will vary.*

G. 1. DB (*Deutsche Bundesbahn*)   2. new train station in Berlin   3. *(internationale) Züge*
   4. Hamburg   5. *Doppeldecker (Bus)*   6. *zwei*   7. 26 euros

Audio CD Program Manager

Content	Textbook Page	Audio CD Number	Track	Time
Unit 1 Begrüßungen und Höflichkeit *(Greetings and Expressions of Courtesy)*	**1**			
Activity 1	2	1	1	1:11
Activity 2	2–3	1	2	1:47
Activity 3	3	1	3	2:43
Activity 4	2	1	4	0:42
Activity 5	2	1	5	0:48
Activity 6	2	1	6	3:01
Activity 7	2	1	7	1:46
Sprichwort	7	1	8	0:18
Unit 2 Die Klasse und Imperative *(Classroom Objects and Commands)*	**13**			
Activity 1	14	1	9	2:28
Activity 2	14	1	10	3:43
Activity 3	15	1	11	1:12
Activity 4	14	1	12	4:33
Activity 5	14	1	13	3:10
Activity 6	15	1	14	4:02
Activity 7	15	1	15	1:23
Sprichwort	23	1	16	0:27
Unit 3 Die Zahlen *(Numbers)*	**29**			
Activity 1	30	1	17	3:26
Activity 2	30	1	18	1:29
Activity 3	30	1	19	1:50
Activity 4	30	1	20	2:17
Activity 5	30	1	21	2:02
Sprichwort	37	1	22	0:18
Unit 4 Die Geografie *(Geography)*	**41**			
Activity 1	42	1	23	1:07
Activity 2	42	1	24	1:03
Activity 3	42	1	25	0:31
Activity 4	42	1	26	0:18
Activity 5	42	1	27	2:26
Sprichwort	55	1	28	0:18

Content	Textbook Page	Audio CD Number	Track	Time
Unit 5 Das Haus *(House)*	**59**			
Activity 1	60	1	29	0:46
Activity 2	60	1	30	1:00
Activity 3	60	1	31	0:46
Activity 4	61	1	32	0:36
Activity 5	60	1	33	1:28
Activity 6	60–61	1	34	2:12
Sprichwort	65	1	35	0:22
Unit 6 Die Familie *(Family)*	**71**			
Activity 1	72	2	1	1:42
Activity 2	73	2	2	0:59
Activity 3	73	2	3	0:44
Activity 4	74	2	4	0:36
Activity 5	72	2	5	1:04
Activity 6	72	2	6	1:09
Activity 7	73	2	7	2:22
Sprichwort	81	2	8	0:21
Unit 7 Die Tiere *(Animals)*	**85**			
Activity 1	86	2	9	0:47
Activity 2	86	2	10	1:38
Activity 3	86	2	11	0:33
Activity 4	87	2	12	0:37
Activity 5	87	2	13	1:09
Activity 6	87	2	14	1:28
Activity 7	86	2	15	1:42
Sprichwort	93	2	16	0:25
Unit 8 Die Berufe *(Occupations)*	**97**			
Activity 1	98	2	17	2:10
Activity 2	98	2	18	1:47
Activity 3	98	2	19	0:50
Activity 4	98	2	20	1:47
Activity 5	98	2	21	1:42
Activity 6	98	2	22	2:25
Sprichwort	107	2	23	0:20

Content	Textbook Page	Audio CD Number	Track	Time
Unit 9 Das Essen *(Food)*	**111**			
Activity 1	112	2	24	2:12
Activity 2	112	2	25	1:24
Activity 3	112	2	26	3:02
Activity 4	113	2	27	1:22
Activity 5	113	2	28	1:13
Activity 6	113	2	29	1:58
Activity 7	115	2	30	0:35
Activity 8	114–115	2	31	1:03
Sprichwort	119	2	32	0:19
Unit 10 Die Kunst *(Art)*	**125**			
Activity 1	126–129	2	33	2:25
Sprichwort	133	2	34	0:19
Unit 11 Der Körper und die Gesundheit *(Body and Health)*	**139**			
Activity 1	140	3	1	1:32
Activity 2	141	3	2	1:19
Activity 3	141	3	3	1:06
Activity 4	141	3	4	1:10
Activity 5	141	3	5	0:43
Activity 6	140–141	3	6	2:17
Activity 7	147	3	7	2:05
Sprichwort	149	3	8	0:20
Unit 12 Die Kleidung *(Clothing)*	**153**			
Activity 1	154–155	3	9	2:14
Activity 2	154	3	10	1:35
Activity 3	155	3	11	0:42
Activity 4	155	3	12	2:54
Activity 5	155	3	13	1:19
Activity 6	154–155	3	14	1:54
Activity 7	160	3	15	1:32
Sprichwort	161	3	16	0:20

Content	Textbook Page	Audio CD Number	Track	Time
Unit 13 Die Zeit und die Farben *(Time and Colors)*	**167**			
Activity 1	167	3	17	5:42
Activity 2	168	3	18	1:22
Activity 3	168	3	19	0:59
Activity 4	169	3	20	0:39
Activity 5	169	3	21	1:24
Activity 6	169	3	22	3:04
Activity 7	168–169	3	23	4:48
Sprichwort	177	3	24	0:18
Unit 14 Die Musik *(Music)*	**183**			
Activity 1	184–185	3	25	0:36
Sprichwort	191	3	26	0:18
Unit 15 Das Wetter und die Jahreszeiten *(Weather and Seasons)*	**195**			
Activity 1	196–197	3	27	1:56
Activity 2	196	3	28	1:40
Activity 3	196–197	3	29	0:39
Activity 4	197	3	30	0:28
Activity 5	197	3	31	1:18
Activity 6	197	3	32	1:27
Sprichwort	203	3	33	0:18
Unit 16 Die Tage und die Monate *(Days and Months)*	**209**			
Activity 1	210	4	1	2:23
Activity 2	210	4	2	2:05
Activity 3	210	4	3	1:54
Activity 4	211	4	4	2:46
Activity 5	211	4	5	0:34
Activity 6	211	4	6	1:11
Sprichwort	219	4	7	0:27
Unit 17 Die Literatur *(Literature)*	**223**			
Activity 1	224–226	4	8	2:51
Activity 2	224–226	4	9	1:48
Sprichwort	229	4	10	0:20

Content	Textbook Page	Audio CD Number	Track	Time
Unit 18 Die Freizeit *(Leisure and Recreation)*	**235**			
Activity 1	236	4	11	1:27
Activity 2	237	4	12	1:28
Activity 3	238	4	13	1:56
Activity 4	236	4	14	1:25
Activity 5	238	4	15	0:59
Activity 6	238	4	16	1:42
Activity 7	242	4	17	0:45
Sprichwort	245	4	18	0:19
Unit 19 Das Einkaufen *(Shopping)*	**249**			
Activity 1	250–251	4	19	3:00
Activity 2	250–251	4	20	1:48
Activity 3	250	4	21	1:29
Activity 4	251	4	22	1:55
Activity 5	251	4	23	2:14
Activity 6	251	4	24	1:47
Activity 7	251	4	25	1:55
Sprichwort	257	4	26	0:24
Unit 20 Das Reisen und der Verkehr *(Travel and Transportation)*	**261**			
Activity 1	262	4	27	0:54
Activity 2	262	4	28	2:19
Activity 3	263	4	29	1:11
Activity 4	263	4	30	1:31
Activity 5	264	4	31	1:01
Activity 6	264	4	32	0:59
Activity 7	264	4	33	1:17
Sprichwort	269	4	34	0:16

Audio Script

Begrüßungen und Höflichkeit
Greetings and Expressions of Courtesy

(1) You will hear several greetings and expressions in German. Listen and repeat each one. *Hör zu und wiederhole!* Are you ready? Let's begin.

Bitte. / Danke. / Bitte schön. / Entschuldigung! / Es tut mir leid. / Viel Glück! / Guten Morgen! / Guten Tag! / Guten Abend! / Gute Nacht! / Ja. / Nein. /

(2) Now you will hear a few short dialogues. Listen carefully. *Hör zu!*

Dialogue 1
Speaker 1: Wie heißt du?
Speaker 2: Ich heiße Alex.
Speaker 1: Angenehm. Es freut mich.

Dialogue 2
Speaker 1: Du sprichst deutsch, nicht wahr?
Speaker 2: Ja. Ich spreche deutsch.

Dialogue 3
Speaker 1: Wie geht's?
Speaker 2: Gut, danke. Und dir?
Speaker 1: Nicht schlecht.

Dialogue 4
Speaker 1: Sprichst du italienisch?
Speaker 2: Nein. Ich spreche nicht italienisch.

The next set of words that you will practice is a list of nine languages. The word for language is *die Sprache*. Say *"die Sprache."* The plural form is *die Sprachen*. Say *"die Sprachen."* Are you ready to repeat? Here we go!

Deutsch / Arabisch / Chinesisch / Französisch / Englisch / Italienisch / Japanisch / Portugiesisch / Russisch / Spanisch /

(3) Now listen to some names of girls and boys. We'll start first with *Mädchennamen*. Repeat after the speaker. *Hör zu und wiederhole!*

Mädchennamen / Ich heiße . . . / Antje / Beate / Bettina / Claudia / Diana / Elisabeth / Gabriele / Heike / Johanna / Julia / Katharina / Laura / Leonie / Marie / Nele / Petra / Ruth / Sabine / Susanne / Vanessa / Das Mädchen heißt Katharina. /

Next we have the boy's names, *Jungennamen*. You know what to do now. Let's start!

Jungennamen / Ich heiße . . . / Alexander / Andreas / Benjamin / Daniel / Dieter / Eberhard / Florian / Günther / Heiko / Jochen / Karsten / Leon / Lukas / Maximilian / Niklas / Paul / Rainer / Stefan / Simon / Tim / Der Junge heißt Paul. /

(4) You will hear three questions in English. In the pause after each one, give the German equivalent. Repeat the response provided.

1. What's your name?
   Wie heißt du?
2. How are you?
   Wie geht's?
3. Do you speak English?
   Sprichst du englisch?

(5) You will hear three questions. This time you must answer each question in German. A speaker will say the answer afterwards so that you can tell whether or not your answer was correct.

1. Wie heißt du?
   Ich heiße . . . *(your name)*
2. Wie geht's?
   Gut, danke. Und dir?
3. Sprichst du englisch?
   Ja. Ich spreche englisch.

(6) You will now hear ten different situations. In the pause after each one, supply an appropriate German expression. Repeat the correct response.

1. It's time to go to bed. What do you say to your father and mother?
   Gute Nacht!
2. Your friend is about to go skiing for the first time. How do you express your hope that she will be successful?
   Viel Glück!
3. You have just spilled milk on the new rug. How do you express your dismay and sorrow?
   Es tut mir leid.
4. Your neighbors are about to go out for dinner and a movie. How do you wish them a pleasant evening?
   Guten Abend!
5. You would like your father or mother to take you to an amusement park next weekend. What special word can you say that just might make this possible?
   Bitte.
6. Your parent has told you that a trip to the amusement park is planned for Saturday. You are very happy! What do you say to your parent?
   Danke.
7. Your parent was pleased to plan the outing and was delighted to hear such a courteous response from you. How does he respond?
   Bitte schön.

8. On your way to school one morning, you pass your neighbor, Mrs. Müller. Say hello to her.
   Guten Morgen, Frau Müller!
9. Later that day you see your German teacher, Mr. Schmidt. You greet him.
   Guten Tag, Herr Schmidt!
10. As you go into your classroom, you see your friend, Bobby. Say hi to him.
    Tag, Bobby!

7 You will hear ten questions in English. In the pause provided, answer each one with either *Ja* or *Nein*. After your response you will hear the right answer.

1. Is a rose a kind of flower?
   Ja.
2. Does a fire hydrant contain fire?
   Nein.
3. Does a thermometer measure temperature?
   Ja.
4. Do you smile when you are happy?
   Ja.
5. Do you say *Viel Glück* when you want to ask for something?
   Nein.
6. Do you ask *Wie geht's?* when you want to know someone's name?
   Nein.
7. Is Heike a name for a *Mädchen?*
   Ja.
8. Is Vanessa a name for a *Junge?*
   Nein.
9. Is *deutsch* spoken in Germany?
   Ja.
10. Is *italienisch* spoken in China?
    Nein.

Sprichwort

Höflichkeit ist Trumpf.
Wiederhole!
Höflichkeit / ist Trumpf. /

Unit 2

Die Klasse und Imperative
Classroom Objects and Commands

1 Listen carefully as the speaker pronounces a word or phrase. Immediately afterwards there will be a pause for you to repeat each word or phrase. *Hör zu und wiederhole!* You may wish to open your book to page 14. Are you ready? Let's begin.

Was ist das? / Das ist ein . . . / Das ist eine . . . / Ist das ein . . . ? / Ist das eine . . . ? /
eine Uhr / ein Bild / eine Tafel / ein Bleistift / ein Wischer / ein Filzstift / ein Drucker /
ein Buch / ein Bücherschrank / ein Klassenzimmer / eine Wand / eine Fahne / ein Fenster /
ein Bildschirm / ein Computer / eine Tastatur / ein Stuhl / eine Maus / ein Blatt Papier /
ein Kuli / ein Heft / eine CD / ein Lineal / eine Landkarte / eine DVD / ein Papierkorb /
ein Schreibtisch /

2 For this activity open your book to page 14. You will now hear the names of 25 classroom objects. As you hear each item, find it and put your finger on it.

1. ein Fenster	10. ein Schreibtisch	19. ein Stuhl
2. ein Bild	11. ein Buch	20. ein Papierkorb
3. ein Computer	12. ein Bleistift	21. eine Uhr
4. eine DVD	13. ein Lineal	22. ein Kuli
5. eine Tastatur	14. ein Heft	23. eine Landkarte
6. eine CD	15. ein Filzstift	24. ein Wischer
7. eine Maus	16. eine Tafel	25. eine Wand
8. ein Bildschirm	17. ein Bücherschrank	
9. ein Drucker	18. ein Blatt Papier	

3 Now we come to the classroom commands. Listen and repeat. *Hör zu und wiederhole!*

Sag das auf Deutsch! / Sprich! / Wiederhole! / Schreib! / Beantworte die Frage! / Geh an die Tafel! / Heb die Hand! / Nimm Papier heraus! / Mach das Buch auf! / Mach das Buch zu! / Zeichne ein Bild! / Ergänze die Sätze! / Hör zu! / Lies! / Schalte den Computer an! / Schalte den Computer aus! /

4 Now you are going to answer the question *"Was ist das?"* Be sure to repeat each correct response provided by the speaker.

Beispiele:	You hear: *Was ist das? (ein Schreibtisch)*
	You say: *Das ist ein Schreibtisch.*
	You hear: *Was ist das? (eine Fahne)*
	You say: *Das ist eine Fahne.*

1. Was ist das? (ein Bild)
   Das ist ein Bild.
2. Was ist das? (ein Computer)
   Das ist ein Computer.
3. Was ist das? (eine DVD)
   Das ist eine DVD.
4. Was ist das? (eine Tastatur)
   Das ist eine Tastatur.
5. Was ist das? (eine Maus)
   Das ist eine Maus.
6. Was ist das? (ein Bildschirm)
   Das ist ein Bildschirm.
7. Was ist das? (ein Drucker)
   Das ist ein Drucker.

8. Was ist das? (ein Lineal)
   Das ist ein Lineal.
9. Was ist das? (ein Filzstift)
   Das ist ein Filzstift.
10. Was ist das? (eine Tafel)
    Das ist eine Tafel.
11. Was ist das? (ein Bücherschrank)
    Das ist ein Bücherschrank.
12. Was ist das? (ein Papierkorb)
    Das ist ein Papierkorb.
13. Was ist das? (eine Landkarte)
    Das ist eine Landkarte.
14. Was ist das? (ein Wischer)
    Das ist ein Wischer.
15. Was ist das? (ein Fenster)
    Das ist ein Fenster.

5 You will hear a brief description of an object, either something about its function or its appearance. Identify the object by its German name. After you give your answer, you will hear the correct answer which you will repeat. For fun, keep track of how many you get right!

> **Beispiel:** This object is used to write on a dry erase board.
> *Das ist ein Filzstift.*

1. This object prints out something from the computer.
   Das ist ein Drucker.
2. This object is used for writing. It has a flat surface.
   Das ist ein Schreibtisch.
3. This object is a place to throw discarded paper.
   Das ist ein Papierkorb.
4. This object writes mostly in black or blue, but sometimes in other colors, too.
   Das ist ein Kuli.
5. This object can be torn out of a notebook.
   Das ist ein Blatt Papier.
6. This object is a straight-edge; it is used to make straight lines and to measure.
   Das ist ein Lineal.
7. This little object is used to tell the computer what to do.
   Das ist eine Maus.
8. This object is the computer's window.
   Das ist ein Bildschirm.
9. This object shows us where cities and countries are.
   Das ist eine Landkarte.
10. This object is a storage place for books.
    Das ist ein Bücherschrank.

6 You are in charge today! Tell a classmate to carry out a certain task. First give the command, then listen to check whether your command was right. Repeat the correct response.

> **Beispiel:** Tell Heike to repeat the sentence.
> *Heike, wiederhole den Satz!*

1. Tell Andreas to speak.
   Andreas, sprich!
2. Tell Bettina to say it in German.
   Bettina, sag das auf Deutsch!
3. Tell Dieter to turn on the computer.
   Dieter, schalte den Computer an!
4. Tell Marie to answer the question.
   Marie, beantworte die Frage!
5. Tell Tim to raise his hand.
   Tim, heb die Hand!
6. Tell Gisela to take out paper.
   Gisela, nimm Papier heraus!
7. Tell David to open the book.
   David, mach das Buch auf!
8. Tell Antje to close the notebook.
   Antje, mach das Heft zu!
9. Tell Karin to turn off the computer.
   Karin, schalte den Computer aus!
10. Tell Karsten to listen.
    Karsten, hör zu!
11. Tell Anna to read.
    Anna, lies!
12. Tell Sabine to draw a picture.
    Sabine, zeichne ein Bild!
13. Tell Rüdiger to complete the sentences.
    Rüdiger, ergänze die Sätze!
14. Tell Heike to go to the board.
    Heike, geh an die Tafel!

(7) In the next activity you will hear five incomplete commands in German. Complete each sentence by supplying the last word that is missing. You will hear the correct answer which you will repeat.

> **Beispiel:** Ergänze die Sätze auf . . . !
> Ergänze die Sätze auf Deutsch!

1. Gerhard, heb die . . . !
   Gerhard, heb die Hand!
2. Heiko, geh an die . . . !
   Heiko, geh an die Tafel!
3. Martina, beantworte die . . . !
   Martina, beantworte die Frage!
4. Tanja, hör . . . !
   Tanja, hör zu!
5. Peter, zeichne ein . . . !
   Peter, zeichne ein Bild.

Sprichwort

Was Hänschen nicht lernt, lernt Hans nimmermehr.
Wiederhole!
Was Hänschen / nicht lernt, / lernt Hans / nimmermehr. /

Unit 3
Die Zahlen
Numbers

1 You're now going to practice the numbers in German. You might like to follow along in your book. Open your book to page 30. Listen and repeat as you look at the numbers 1 to 19. *Hör zu und wiederhole!*

> eins / zwei / drei / vier / fünf / sechs / sieben / acht / neun / zehn / elf / zwölf / dreizehn / vierzehn / fünfzehn / sechzehn / siebzehn / achtzehn / neunzehn /

Now we'll go to the next group, numbers 20 to 29. *Hör zu und wiederhole!*

> zwanzig / einundzwanzig / zweiundzwanzig / dreiundzwanzig / vierundzwanzig / fünfundzwanzig / sechsundzwanzig / siebenundzwanzig / achtundzwanzig / neunundzwanzig /

The numbers 30 to 99 have a common pattern. *Hör zu und wiederhole!*

> dreißig / einunddreißig / zweiunddreißig / vierzig / einundvierzig /zweiundvierzig /

Now repeat counting by tens and the word for "hundred" and "thousand." *Hör zu und wiederhole!*

> zehn / zwanzig / dreißig / vierzig / fünfzig / sechzig / siebzig / achtzig / neunzig / hundert / tausend /

2 Now it's time for you to count. Listen to the first group, 1 to 5. Then repeat all the numbers consecutively.

> eins, zwei, drei, vier, fünf /

The next group is 6 to 10. Listen to the numbers and then repeat all the numbers as a group.

> sechs, sieben, acht, neun, zehn /

Now you will hear the numbers 11 to 19. Listen to the entire group. Then, in the pause provided, repeat all the numbers consecutively. *Hör zu und wiederhole!*

> elf, zwölf, dreizehn, vierzehn, fünfzehn, sechzehn, siebzehn, achtzehn, neunzehn /

3 Now, instead of repeating, you have to say what number you hear. For example, you hear *vierundsiebzig* and you say "seventy-four." There will be two numbers representing each group of ten. You can find out whether you guessed correctly when you hear the answer afterwards. Are you ready?

sieben	*sechsundfünfzig*
seven	fifty-six
drei	*achtundsechzig*
three	sixty-eight
vierzehn	*neunundsiebzig*
fourteen	seventy-nine
sechzehn	*zweiundachtzig*
sixteen	eighty-two
einundzwanzig	*achtundneunzig*
twenty-one	ninety-eight
neununddreißig	*dreihundert*
thirty-nine	three hundred
siebenundvierzig	*tausend*
forty-seven	one thousand

(4) This time, you will hear a number in English and you say it in German. After your response, you'll hear the correct German word which you will repeat.

one / *eins*	forty-six / *sechsundvierzig*
three / *drei*	fifty-nine / *fünfundneunzig*
eight / *acht*	sixty-four / *vierundsechzig*
ten / *zehn*	seventy-one / *einundsiebzig*
twelve / *zwölf*	eighty-eight / *achtundachtzig*
fifteen / *fünfzehn*	ninety-three / *dreiundneunzig*
twenty-seven / *siebenundzwanzig*	one hundred / *hundert*
thirty-two / *zweiunddreißig*	

(5) Let's do a little arithmetic *"auf Deutsch."* Try to add, subtract, multiply, and divide. Listen to the example and then do the math problems. Repeat each correct answer.

> **Beispiel:** *Wie viel ist zwei und zwei?*
> *Vier. Zwei und zwei ist vier.*

1. *Wie viel ist zwei und neun?*
   Elf. Zwei und neun ist elf.
2. *Wie viel ist achtzehn weniger zehn?*
   Acht. Achtzehn weniger zehn ist acht.
3. *Wie viel ist fünfzig mal zwei?*
   Hundert. Fünfzig mal zwei ist hundert.
4. *Wie viel ist hundert geteilt durch fünf?*
   Zwanzig. Hundert geteilt durch fünf ist zwanzig.

Sprichwort

Jede Münze hat zwei Seiten.
Wiederhole!
Jede Münze / hat zwei Seiten. /

Unit 4

Die Geografie
Geography

1 Listen to the names of the following cities and then repeat each one. You may want to look at the map on page 42. *Hör zu und wiederhole!*

Berlin / Hamburg / Köln / Leipzig / Dresden / München / Frankfurt / Wien / Zürich / Vaduz / Bern / Gstaad / Sankt Moritz / Genf /

2 Now repeat the German names of Germany, Switzerland and Austria, and the countries that border them.

Deutschland / die Schweiz / Österreich / Liechtenstein / Dänemark / die Niederlande / Belgien / Luxemburg / Frankreich / Italien / Slowenien / Ungarn / die Tschechische Republik / die Slowakische Republik / Polen /

3 Finally, repeat the names of these bodies of water and mountain ranges:

die Nordsee / die Ostsee / der Rhein / die Elbe / die Donau / der Harz / die Alpen /

4 Now you will hear the locations of ten cities. In each case you are to guess the name of the city. You might like to look at your map on page 42. After you have had a chance to decide, you will hear the correct answer.

1. This city is located on the *Donau* or Danube River in Austria.
   Wien
2. This city is located in northeastern Germany.
   Berlin
3. This city is located in the southern part of Germany.
   München
4. This city is located at the western edge of Lake Geneva in Switzerland.
   Genf
5. This city is located on the Main River in central Germany
   Frankfurt
6. This city is located in Austria close to the border of Germany.
   Salzburg
7. This city is located in northern Germany.
   Hamburg
8. This city is located northwest of Dresden.
   Leipzig
9. This capital city is located between Switzerland and Austria.
   Vaduz
10. This city is located in northern Switzerland.
    Zürich

(5) Can you answer these questions? Take a few moments to think and then give a short answer. You will then hear the correct answer.

1. In what part of Germany is the Harz Mountain Range?
   Central
2. What small country lies between Switzerland and Austria?
   Liechtenstein
3. What river starts in southern Germany and flows eastward?
   The Danube (or *Donau*)
4. What country is situated between *die Tschechische Republik* and *Slowenien?*
   Austria (or *Österreich*)
5. Into what body of water does the Elbe River flow?
   The North Sea (or *die Nordsee*).
6. In what country can you find these places: Gstaad and Sankt Moritz?
   Switzerland *(die Schweiz)*
7. The Elbe is a *Fluss*. What is the English meaning of a *Fluss*?
   River
8. On how many countries does Lake Contance border?
   Three
9. Is the Netherlands situated to the east or west of Germany?
   West
10. Is Hungary situated to the east or west of Austria?
    East

Sprichwort

Andere Länder, andere Sitten.
Wiederhole!
Andere Länder, / andere Sitten. /

Unit 5

Das Haus
House

 Katja, Michael, Mahmood, and Sophie are curious about their friends' houses. Each of them has a question for a friend. Listen now to the questions and answers. *Hör zu!*

KATJA	Wo wohnst du?
JULIA:	Ich wohne in einem Haus in Köln.
MICHAEL:	Wo ist der Garten?
JOHANN:	Der Garten ist da drüben.

MAHMOOD:	Wo ist die Garage?
HALIMA:	Sie ist hinter dem Garten.

SOPHIE:	Wie viele Zimmer gibt es in deinem Haus?
LISBETH:	Es gibt acht Zimmer.

2 It is now your turn to answer these questions. See if you can answer them without looking at your book. As usual, you will hear each correct answer which you will repeat.

Wo wohnst du?
Ich wohne in einem Haus in Köln.

Wo ist der Garten?
Der Garten ist da drüben.

Wo ist die Garage?
Sie ist hinter dem Garten.

Wie viele Zimmer gibt es in deinem Haus?
Es gibt acht Zimmer.

3 On page 60 you will see a floor plan of a house. Listen and repeat the words. *Hör zu und wiederhole!*

die Terrasse / das Schlafzimmer / das WC / die Küche / das Badezimmer / das Wohnzimmer / das Esszimmer / der Garten / die Garage /

4 Here are a few more places to stay. *Hör zu und wiederhole!*

die Villa / das Einfamilienhaus / das Mietshaus / die Wohnung / die Eigentumswohnung / die Hütte / das Zelt /

5 You will now hear five sentences, all of which have the last word missing. In the pause provided, complete each sentence with the correct German room. A clue in English will help you. After you try, you will hear the final version.

> **Beispiel:** You hear: taking a bath
> You hear the incomplete sentence: *Ich bade in dem . . .*
>
> You say: *Badezimmer*

1. relaxing/entertaining guests
   Ich entspanne mich in dem . . .
   Wohnzimmer
2. cooking
   Ich koche in der . . .
   Küche
3. eating
   Ich esse in dem . . .
   Esszimmer

4. sleeping
   Ich schlafe in dem . . .
   Schlafzimmer
5. playing outside
   Ich spiele in dem . . .
   Garten

(6) Do you think you know your Unit 5 words well enough to identify a few? Try saying these German words and phrases. Repeat the correct answers after the speaker.

1. the yard
   der Garten
2. the apartment building
   das Mietshaus
3. behind the garden
   hinter dem Garten
4. the living room
   das Wohnzimmer
5. how many rooms
   wie viele Zimmer
6. the tent
   das Zelt
7. Where do you live?
   Wo wohnst du?
8. Where is the garage?
   Wo ist die Garage?
9. There are six rooms.
   Es gibt sechs Zimmer.
10. There's no place like home.
    Eigener Herd is Goldes wert.

Sprichwort

Eigener Herd ist Goldes wert.
Wiederhole!
Eigener Herd / ist Goldes wert.

Unit 6

Die Familie
Family

(1) You will now hear the names of some family members. *Hör zu und wiederhole!*

die Großeltern / die Großmutter / der Großvater / die Eltern / der Mann / die Frau / der Vater / die Mutter / der Onkel / die Tante / die Kinder / der Bruder / die Schwester / die Tochter / der Sohn / die Enkelin / der Enkel / die Nichte / der Neffe / die Kusine / der Cousin /

2 Listen to the following conversations that might be overheard at a family reunion. *Hör zu!*

MONIKA:	Wer ist das?
EBERHARD:	Das ist mein Bruder.
JOCHEN:	Wer sind die Kinder?
RUTH:	Sie sind mein Enkel und meine Enkelin.
SUSANNE:	Sind das deine Eltern?
EVELYN:	Ja, meine Mutter heißt Jutta und mein Vater heißt Josef.
CLAUDIA:	Leonie, Sabine, und Alexander sind Schwestern und Bruder, nicht wahr?
MARKUS:	Ja, und sie sind auch meine Cousins.
NIKLAS:	Wo sind deine Verwandten?
SIMON:	Meine Großeltern sind drinnen und meine Tanten und Onkel sind im Garten.
LAURA:	Sind deine Paten hier?
DIETER:	Ja, sicher. Meine Patin spricht gerade mit meinen Tanten. Mein Pate ist auf der Terrasse.

3 Now listen and repeat after the speaker. *Hör zu und wiederhole!*

Vergiss nicht! / Familientreffen / Gäste / Tante Anneliese und ihr Mann / meine Schwester und ihre Kinder / Onkel Willi und seine Frau / Diana und das Baby /

4 Our blended families have some words of their own. *Hör zu und wiederhole!*

der Stiefbruder / die Stiefschwester / der Stiefvater / die Stiefmutter / der Stiefsohn / die Stieftochter /

5 You will hear the German names of six family members. After each pause provided, say the English meaning of each one. The correct answer will be given afterwards.

1. der Onkel
   the uncle
2. die Großmutter
   the grandmother
3. die Tante
   the aunt
4. der Großvater
   the grandfather
5. der Neffe
   the nephew
6. die Kusine
   the cousin

6 *Wer ist das?* Guess who each person is. Answer in German. After you try, the correct answer will be given.

1. Die Schwester von meiner Mutter ist meine . . .
   Tante

2. Der Bruder von meinem Vater ist mein . . .
   Onkel
3. Der Sohn von meiner Mutter ist mein . . .
   Bruder
4. Der Vater von meiner Mutter ist mein . . .
   Großvater
5. Die Tochter von meinem Onkel ist meine . . .
   Kusine

(7) The following exercise has questions about "how many" and "who." Answer each question in German. Use the cue. After you try, you'll hear the correct answer which you will repeat. Let's start.

1. Wie viele Kinder gibt es in der Familie? (fünf)
   Es gibt fünf Kinder in der Familie.
2. Wie viele Familien wohnen in dem Mietshaus? (zwölf)
   Zwölf Familien wohnen in dem Mietshaus.
3. Wie viele Brüder hast du? (drei)
   Ich habe drei Brüder.
4. Wie viele Großmütter hast du? (zwei)
   Ich habe zwei Großmütter.
5. Wer ist der Junge auf der Terrasse? (mein Bruder)
   Das ist mein Bruder.
6. Wer ist die Frau in dem Wohnzimmer? (meine Tante Angelika)
   Das ist meine Tante Angelika.
7. Wer sind die Männer in dem Garten? (mein Vater und mein Pate)
   Sie sind mein Vater und mein Pate.

Sprichwort

Der Apfel fällt nicht weit vom Stamm.
Wiederhole!
Der Apfel / fällt nicht weit / vom Stamm. /

Unit 7

Die Tiere
Animals

(1) Listen and repeat the name of each animal in the pause provided. *Hör zu und wiederhole!*

die Kuh / der Esel / der Vogel / die Ente / das Schwein / der Hahn / die Henne / die Katze / das Pferd / der Hund /

(2) Let's review that list. This time, say the corresponding German word after you hear the English name. Listen and repeat the German word after the speaker.

cow / *die Kuh,* horse / *das Pferd,* donkey / *der Esel,* duck / *die Ente,* dog / *der Hund,* cat / *die Katze,* pig / *das Schwein,* bird / *der Vogel,* hen / *die Henne,* rooster / *der Hahn*

(3) Listen to the conversation between Jutta and Simon that takes place on a farm. *Hör zu!*

JUTTA:	Komm mit, Simon! Ich füttre jetzt die Tiere. Ich gebe Max einen Apfel.
SIMON:	Schön! Ich möchte helfen.
JUTTA:	Ja, sicher, Simon. Du kannst den Eimer halten.
SIMON:	Wie heißt die Katze?
JUTTA:	Das ist Miezi.
SIMON:	Gibt es auch Hennen?
JUTTA:	Ja, viele! Sie sind hinter der Scheune. Du kannst die Eier sammeln.

(4) Here are some phrases indicating locations. They tell where some animals are. *Hör zu und wiederhole!*

auf dem Lande / in der Luft / auf der Weide / in der Scheune / auf dem Teich / im Stall /

(5) This time we'll reverse the phrases. After you hear each English phrase, give the German equivalent. Of course, you will then hear the German response which you should repeat.

in the country / *auf dem Lande*
on the pond / *auf dem Teich*
in the field / *auf der Weide*
in the stable / *im Stall*
in the barn / *in der Scheune*
in the air / *in der Luft*

(6) The last two dialogues take place at the farm. Listen to both dialogues. *Hör zu!*

JUTTA:	Was machst du, Simon?
SIMON:	Ich sammle die Eier.
SIMON:	Was machst du, Jutta?
JUTTA:	Ich streichle mein Kaninchen.

Do you remember what the children are doing? *Sag das auf Deutsch!*

1. What is Simon is gathering?
   die Eier
2. What is Jutta petting?
   das Kaninchen
3. How do you ask in German "What are you doing"?
   Was machst du?
4. How do you say in German "I'm gathering the eggs"?
   Ich sammle die Eier.
5. How do you say in German "I'm petting my rabbit"?
   Ich streichle mein Kaninchen.

How well do you think you know these animals? Test your knowledge by answering *ja* or *nein* to each question. Listen afterwards for the correct answer.

1. Is a *Schwein* big?
   Ja.
2. Is a *Vogel* little?
   Ja.
3. Does a *Pferd* fly?
   Nein.
4. Does an *Ente* swim?
   Ja.
5. Does a *Kaninchen* live in a pond?
   Nein.
6. Does a *Ziege* have wings?
   Nein.
7. Is a *Hahn* a type of bird?
   Ja.
8. Can a *Henne* take you for a ride?
   Nein.
9. Does an *Esel* usually rest in a stable?
   Ja.
10. Does the *Kuh* give you eggs?
    Nein.

Sprichwort

Wenn die Katze aus dem Haus ist, tanzen die Mäuse.
Wiederhole!
Wenn die Katze / aus dem Haus ist, / tanzen die Mäuse. /

Unit 8

Die Berufe
Occupations

 You will hear masculine and feminine words for various occupations. *Hör zu und wiederhole!*

der Künstler / die Künstlerin / der Geschäftsmann / die Geschäftsfrau / der Elektriker / die Elektrikerin / der Tischler / die Tischlerin / der Koch / die Köchin / der Krankenpfleger / die Krankenpflegerin / der Mechaniker / die Mechanikerin / der Arzt / die Ärztin / der Musiker / die Musikerin / der Lehrer / die Lehrerin / der Landwirt / die Landwirtin / der Briefträger / die Briefträgerin / der Klempner / die Klempnerin / der Programmierer / die Programmiererin /

2 Listen to four short dialogues about what people do for a living. Listen and then repeat each line in the time provided. *Hör zu!*

1. Wo arbeitest du?
   Ich arbeite auf dem Lande. Ich bin Landwirt.

2. Arbeitest du gern?
   Ja. Ich arbeite gern.

3. Was machst du?
   Ich bin Schauspielerin. Ich arbeite im Theater.

4. Was ist dein Beruf?
   Ich bin Schauspieler.

Now repeat after the speaker. *Wiederhole!*

1. Wo arbeitest du? /
   Ich arbeite auf dem Lande. / Ich bin Landwirt. /

2. Arbeitest du gern? /
   Ja. Ich arbeite gern. /

3. Was machst du? /
   Ich bin Schauspielerin. / Ich arbeite im Theater. /

4. Was ist dein Beruf? /
   Ich bin Schauspieler. /

3 Listen to six short dialogues. In each one you will hear two different ways of asking a friend what he or she does for a living. For each job or profession you will hear the way a man says his job title and the way a woman says hers. Listen closely. *Hör gut zu!*

Speaker 1: *Was ist dein Beruf?*
Speaker 2: *Ich bin Schauspieler.*

Speaker 1: *Was machst du?*
Speaker 2: *Ich bin Schauspielerin.*

Speaker 1: *Was ist dein Beruf?*
Speaker 2: *Ich bin Künstler.*

Speaker 1: *Was machst du?*
Speaker 2: *Ich bin Künstlerin.*

Speaker 1: *Was ist dein Beruf?*
Speaker 2: *Ich bin Briefträger.*

Speaker 1: *Was machst du?*
Speaker 2: *Ich bin Briefträgerin.*

(4) Say what each person's profession is according to the word cue. Listen to the example. Repeat each correct response.

> **Beispiel:** You hear: Herr Maier / Geschäftsmann
> You say: Herr Maier ist Geschäftsmann.

1. Willi / Krankenpfleger
   Willi ist Krankenpfleger.
2. Heidi / Schauspielerin
   Heidi ist Schauspielerin.
3. Susi / Ärztin
   Susi ist Ärztin.
4. Herr Schmidt / Landwirt
   Herr Schmidt ist Landwirt.
5. Frau Ellermann / Mechanikerin
   Frau Ellermann ist Mechanikerin.

(5) And now in the negative, state what the person's profession is not. Repeat the correct response.

> **Beispiele:** Peter / kein Arzt
> Peter ist kein Arzt.
>
> Anna / keine Elektrikerin
> Anna ist keine Elektrikerin.

1. Jochen / kein Klempner
   Jochen ist kein Klempner.
2. Petra / keine Musikerin
   Petra ist keine Musikerin.
3. Der Mann / kein Künstler
   Der Mann ist kein Künstler.
4. Die Frau / keine Lehrerin
   Die Frau ist keine Lehrerin.
5. Daniel / kein Tischler
   Daniel ist kein Tischler.

(6) Show how well you can remember the job titles of women and men. You will hear a sentence followed by a word cue indicating a particular person. Use that new person as you revise the sentence. Repeat each correct answer.

> **Beispiel:** You hear: Mein Großvater ist Koch. (meine Großmutter)
> You say: Meine Großmutter ist Köchin.

1. Mein Freund ist Künstler. (meine Freundin)
   Meine Freundin ist Künstlerin.
2. Mein Vater ist Lehrer. (meine Mutter)
   Meine Mutter ist Lehrerin.
3. Meine Tante ist Ärztin.(mein Onkel)
   Mein Onkel ist Arzt.

4. Mein Bruder ist Elektriker. (meine Schwester)
   Meine Schwester ist Elektrikerin.
5. Meine Kusine ist Briefträgerin. (mein Cousin)
   Mein Cousin ist Briefträger.
6. Holger ist Programmierer. (Heidi)
   Heidi ist Programmiererin.

Sprichwort

Erst die Arbeit, dann das Vergnügen.
Wiederhole!
Erst die Arbeit, / dann das Vergnügen. /

Unit 9

Das Essen
Food

 Listen and repeat the following words and phrases. *Hör zu und wiederhole!*

die Zitronenlimonade / 1,35 Euro (pro Liter) /
die Milch / 1,50 Euro (pro Liter) /
der Orangensaft / 1,50 Euro (pro Liter) /
das Mineralwasser / 1 Euro (pro Liter) /
die Limonade / 2 Euro (pro Liter)

Now listen to the English words and supply the German equivalents. You will hear each German word which you are to repeat.

soda or soda drink / *die Limonade*
mineral water / *das Mineralwasser*
milk / *die Milch*
orange juice / *der Orangensaft*
lemonade / *die Zitronenlimonade*

2 Not far from *Lisbeths Lebensmittel* is a small restaurant with a reputation for excellent regional food. It's called *Eberhards Ecke* or Eberhard's Corner. Listen to the words and repeat them. *Hör zu und wiederhole!*

Eberhards Ecke / Ländliche Küche / Tagesgericht / Mittwoch / Frühstücksangebot / Europäisch / Hörnchen und Saft / freie Wahl / Bauer / zwei Eier / Schinken oder Wurst / Toastbrot / Röstkartoffeln und Orangensaft / Bei uns schmeckt's immer! /

3 Now you will hear some short conversations. First listen and then repeat after the speaker the second time around. *Hör zu!*

Was gibt's zu essen?
Es gibt Suppe und Salat.

Hast du Hunger?
Ja. Ich habe Hunger.

Was isst du?
Ich esse ein Butterbrot.

Was gibt's zu trinken?
Es gibt Milch.

Hast du Durst, Ali?
Nein. Ich habe keinen Durst.

Was trinkst du, Matthias?
Ich trinke ein Glas Milch.

Now repeat after the speaker. *Wiederhole!*

Was gibt's zu essen? /
Es gibt Suppe und Salat. /

Hast du Hunger? /
Ja. Ich habe Hunger. /

Was isst du? /
Ich esse ein Butterbrot. /

Was gibt's zu trinken? /
Es gibt Milch. /

Hast du Durst, Ali? /
Nein. Ich habe keinen Durst. /

Was trinkst du, Matthias? /
Ich trinke ein Glas Milch. /

Without looking at your book, see if you can answer these same questions. After you have answered each question you will hear the correct answer once more. Repeat it.

Was gibt's zu essen?
Es gibt Suppe und Salat.

Hast du Hunger?
Ja. Ich habe Hunger.

Was isst du?
Ich esse ein Butterbrot.

Was gibt's zu trinken?
Es gibt Milch.

Hast du Durst, Ali?
Nein. Ich habe keinen Durst.

Was trinkst du, Matthias?
Ich trinke ein Glas Milch.

(4) Fruits are part of a healthy diet, so let's pick up some *Obst* at the market! *Hör zu und wiederhole!*

das Obst / die Birne / die Ananas / die Banane / der Apfel / die Apfelsine /

Now answer the next questions by using the cues. Repeat each response.

Was isst du? (eine Banane)
Ich esse eine Banane.

Was isst du? (einen Apfel)
Ich esse einen Apfel.

Was isst du? (das Obst)
Ich esse das Obst.

(5) Listen to the various items that are often found on a dinner table. *Hör zu und wiederhole!*

der Pfeffer / das Salz / die Vase / die Untertasse / die Tasse / das Glas / die Butter / die Serviette / der Teller / die Gabel / das Messer / der Löffel / der Teelöffel / der Zucker / die Tischdecke / der Tisch /

(6) You might find the following items on a shopping list. Listen und repeat each word. *Hör zu und wiederhole!*

die Einkaufsliste / der Spinat / die Tomatensuppe / die Kekse / das Fleisch / die Kartoffeln / die Zwiebeln / das Hähnchen / der Käse / das Brot / der Pudding / das Eis / die Wurst / die grünen Bohnen /

Let's review the meals of the day and some typical foods. Listen and repeat each sentence. *Hör zu und wiederhole!*

Zum Frühstück gibt es Toastbrot, Butter, Marmelade und Saft. /
Zum Mittagessen gibt es Hähnchen, Kartoffeln, Spinat und grüne Bohnen. /
Zum Abendessen gibt es Brot, Suppe und Salat. /

(7) *Guten Appetit!* is a polite little expression that is traditionally said when people sit down for dinner. It is a wish on the part of a friend or the host for all guests to enjoy the meal and eat heartily. Let's say it again. *Guten Appetit!*

You are serving a special dinner to your guests, Herr und Frau Walser. Say their names as you wish them an enjoyable meal . . . *(Guten Appetit, Herr und Frau Walser).*

(8) To conclude this unit we will say the specialties of Germany, Austria, and Switzerland. Some day you may serve one of these specialties to guests and now you will know how to present it to them in German! *Hör zu und wiederhole!*

Schweinebraten / Königsberger Klopse / Strammer Max / Hühnerfrikassee / Spätzle / Leipziger Allerlei / Linseneintopf / Lebkuchen / Erdbeertorte / Stollen /

Hunger ist der beste Koch.
Wiederhole!
Hunger / ist der beste / Koch. /

Unit

Die Kunst
Art

1 You will hear the names of the famous artists and the places they lived or with which they are associated. Then, you will hear where each artist comes from and you will form a sentence using the information given. Repeat each correct answer.

> **Beispiel:**   Albrecht Dürer (Nürnberg)
> Albrecht Dürer kommt aus Nürnberg.

Caspar David Friedrich (Greifswald)
Caspar David Friedrich kommt aus Greifswald. /

Ernst Ludwig Kirchner (Dresden)
Ernst Ludwig Kirchner kommt aus Dresden. /

Franz Marc (München)
Franz Marc kommt aus München. /

Neo Rauch (Leipzig)
Neo Rauch kommt aus Leipzig. /

Gerhard Richter (Dresden)
Gerhard Richter kommt aus Dresden. /

Jutta Votteler (Mainz)
Jutta Votteler kommt aus Mainz. /

Madeleine Dietz (Mannheim)
Madeleine Dietz kommt aus Mannheim. /

Sprichwort

Die Kunst ist lang, das Leben kurz.
Wiederhole!
Die Kunst ist lang, / das Leben kurz. /

Unit 11

Der Körper und die Gesundheit
Body and Health

1 Listen to the following words relating to parts of the body and repeat them. *Hör zu und wiederhole!*

> die Körperteile / der Kopf / das Haar / das Ohr / die Ohren / der Hals / die Schulter / die Brust / der Arm / der Bauch / der Ellenbogen / die Hand / der Finger / das Knie / die Zehe / der Fuß /

2 Now you will hear the names of the parts of the face. *Hör zu und wiederhole!*

> die Gesichtsteile / die Stirn / das Auge / die Augen / die Nase / der Mund / der Zahn / die Zähne / die Lippe / die Lippen / das Kinn /

You will now hear some additional words that you should repeat. *Hör zu und wiederhole!*

> die Gesundheit / wohl / glücklich / krank / ungesund / gesund / traurig /

3 Now provide the German equivalents for the following English words. Then repeat the correct words after the speaker.

> health / *die Gesundheit*
> healthy / *gesund*
> unhealthy / *ungesund*
> sick / *krank*
> well / *wohl*
> sad / *traurig*
> happy / *glücklich*

4 You will now hear four short sentences. Change the last word you hear to its opposite and then say the sentence again with the new word.

> **Beispiel:**   You hear: Ich bin traurig.
> You say: Ich bin glücklich.

> 1. Ich fühle mich krank.
>   Ich fühle mich wohl.
> 2. Willi ist glücklich.
>   Willi ist traurig.
> 3. Beate ist ungesund.
>   Beate ist gesund.
> 4. Es geht mir gut.
>   Es geht mir schlecht.

5 Listen carefully to these dialogues between friends. *Hör zu!*

JASMIN:	Tag, Anja, wie geht's?
ANJA:	Es geht mir schlecht. Ich bin müde.
LISBETH:	Arbeitest du noch?
LUIGI:	Ja. Ich lerne für eine Klassenarbeit morgen.
HALIMA:	Was hast du?
AHMED:	Ich habe Kopfweh.
KARL:	Ist Martina heute krank?
STEFAN:	Ja. Sie hat die Grippe!
NELE:	Wie fühlst du dich?
MARIA:	Ich fühle mich wohl.
JOHANNA:	Bist du traurig, Raimund?
RAIMUND:	Nein. Ich bin glücklich!

6 Now you will hear incomplete sentences in English. In the pause provided, say the missing German word.

1. To look at paintings by Dürer, Friedrich, Kirchner, and Marc I use my . . .
   Augen
2. To hold the baton as I conduct music by Bach, Mozart, and Beethoven I use my . . .
   Hand
3. To think about ideas in books by Goethe and Schiller I use my . . .
   Kopf
4. To smell the enticing aromas coming from the kitchen I use my . . .
   Nase
5. To eat the delicious specialties at *Eberhards Ecke* I use my . . .
   Mund
6. Everyday I floss and brush my . . .
   Zähne
7. To maintain good posture I hold back my . . .
   Schulter
8. By not listening to loud music and noise I protect myself from hearing loss and injury of both of my . . .
   Ohren
9. I do sit-ups to strengthen the muscles in my . . .
   Bauch
10. I use a comb and a brush on my . . .
    Haar

7 Listen now to the reading passage on page 147 (Exercise H) of your textbook. Afterwards you will hear eight incomplete sentences. Finish each one with just one word in German. *Viel Glück!*

Ich heiße Alex. Ich bin vierzehn Jahre alt. Es geht mir gut und ich bin gesund. Ich denke mit dem Kopf. Ich spreche deutsch mit dem Mund. Ich schreibe mit der Hand und ich gehe mit den Beinen und Füßen zur Schule. Ich sehe die Bilder von Dürer mit den Augen. Ich rieche die Blumen im Garten mit der Nase. Ich esse zu Mittag mit den Zähnen. Der Körper ist fantastisch, nicht wahr?

Now, finish these sentences with one word.

1. Es geht mir . . .
   gut
2. Ich denke mit dem . . .
   Kopf
3. Ich spreche deutsch mit dem . . .
   Mund
4. Ich schreibe mit der . . .
   Hand
5. Ich gehe mit den Beinen und . . .
   Füßen
6. Ich sehe die Bilder von Dürer mit den . . .
   Augen
7. Ich rieche die Blumen im Garten mit der . . .
   Nase
8. Ich esse zu Mittag mit den . . .
   Zähnen

Sprichwort

Lachen ist die beste Medizin.
Wiederhole!
Lachen / ist die beste / Medizin. /

Unit 12

Die Kleidung
Clothing

1 A large department store, *Die Neue Mode,* has just about everything you need to be fashionably dressed. You will hear a list of clothing items. We will start with the men's department. *Hör zu und wiederhole!*

Neue Mode / der Pullover / die Hose / die Schuhe / der Schlafanzug / die Socken / der Anzug / die Jacke / das Hemd / die Krawatte / das Taschentuch / die Handschuhe / die Baseball-Mütze / das T-Shirt / die Jeans / die kurze Hose / die Badehose /

Check your memory now and see if you can say the German words for the following items.

socks / *die Socken*
pants or slacks / *die Hose*
shirt / *das Hemd*
gloves / *die Handschuhe*
tie / *die Krawatte*

2 Now here is a selection from the women's department. *Hör zu und wiederhole!*

das Kleid / der Schlafanzug / der Hut / die Bluse / der Gürtel /der Rock / die Schuhe / die Freizeitschuhe / der Bademantel / die Jeans / die kurze Hose / der Badeanzug /

As you did earlier, check your memory now and say the German words for the following items.

shoes / *die Schuhe*
skirt / *der Rock*
dress / *das Kleid*
hat / *der Hut*
belt / *der Gürtel*

3 Listen carefully to the following dialogues about clothing.

HEIKE:	Was hast du an?
RAINER:	Ich habe meinen neuen Anzug an.
HEIKE:	Warum?
RAINER:	Ich gehe heute Abend in ein Konzert.
ANDREAS:	Ich gehe draußen in den Garten.
MARIANNE:	Warte mal. Ich gehe mit. Ich hole aber zuerst meine Jacke.
LAURA:	Wie ist der Mantel?
ANGELIKA:	Er ist schön.
KEMAL:	Was machst du, Marie?
MARIE:	Ich packe meinen Koffer.
KEMAL:	Warum?
MARIA:	Ich reise bald in die Schweiz.
KEMAL:	Vergiss nicht deinen Skianzug!

4 In this next activity you will hear the English parts of the dialogues. Say it all in German! You may use your book, if you think you must peek once in a while. Try, however, not to use it. You will hear the German words afterwards which you should repeat.

What are you doing, Marie?
Was machst du, Marie?

I'm packing my suitcase.
Ich packe meinen Koffer.

Why?
Warum?

I'm traveling to Switzerland soon.
Ich reise bald in die Schweiz.

Don't forget your ski outfit!
Vergiss nicht deinen Skianzug!

I'm going out in the yard.
Ich gehe draußen in den Garten.

Wait a minute. I'm going with you.
Warte mal. Ich gehe mit.

But first I'm going to get my jacket.
Ich hole aber zuerst meine Jacke.

What are you wearing?
Was hast du an?

I'm wearing my new suit.
Ich habe meinen neuen Anzug an.

Why?
Warum?

I'm going to a concert this evening.
Ich gehe heute Abend in ein Konzert.

How is the coat?
Wie ist der Mantel?

It's nice.
Er ist schön.

5 Marie is going on vacation. She is making a list of things she will need in Switzerland during January. *Hör zu und wiederhole!*

Winterferien / Schweiz – Januar / 2 Kleider / 3 Hüte / 1 Schlafanzug / 2 Gürtel / 3 Taschentücher / 1 Jacke / 1 Pulli / 3 Hosen / 3 Hemden / 1 Rock / Mantel / Socken / Schuhe / Handschuhe /

6 What to wear when? After you hear a cue, identify an article of clothing that is appropriate to that situation. You only need to provide the noun without the appropriate forms of *ein* or *der, die, das.*

What do you . . .

1. wear to bed?
   Schlafanzug
2. wear with a blouse?
   Rock
3. wear on the head?
   Hut, Mütze
4. wear to a formal occasion?
   Anzug, Kleid
5. wear on your hands?
   Handschuhe
6. wear with trousers or pants?
   Hemd
7. wear before or after a bath?
   Bademantel

8. wear inside your shoes?
   Socken
9. wear at the neck with a dress shirt?
   Krawatte
10. wear with a skirt?
    Bluse

(7) You will hear the passage on page 160 of your book followed by questions based on that reading. *Hör zu!*

Marie geht mit ihrer Familie in den Urlaub. Sie reist nach Zürich, einer Stadt in der Schweiz. Sie packt ihren Koffer nur mit ihrer Winterkleidung. Sie wählt: zwei Hosen, zwei Pullover, ein Kleid, einen Rock, eine Bluse und eine Jacke. Sie hat alle nötigen Kleidungsstücke für ihren Urlaub in der Schweiz.

Now you will hear five questions. In the pause provided, answer each question with just a name or a German word.

1. Who is going on vacation?
   Marie
2. What city will she visit?
   Zürich
3. What does she pack?
   Koffer
4. In which season will she be traveling?
   Winter
5. How many pairs of pants does she plan to take?
   zwei

Sprichwort

Das Hemd ist mir näher als der Rock.
Wiederhole!
Das Hemd / ist mir näher / als der Rock.

Unit 13

Die Zeit und die Farben
Time and Colors

(1) *Wie viel Uhr ist es?* (What time is it?) You will hear the time expressed in four different groups. Listen to the English first and then give the corresponding German. You will hear the correct words afterwards which you should repeat. *Viel Glück!*

Group 1: the exact hour
It is one o'clock.
Es ist ein Uhr.

It is three o'clock.
Es ist drei Uhr.

It is five o'clock.
Es ist fünf Uhr.

It is seven o'clock.
Es ist sieben Uhr.

It is nine o'clock.
Es ist neun Uhr.

It is eleven o'clock.
Es ist elf Uhr.

It is mid-day, or noon.
Es ist Mittag.

It is midnight.
Es ist Mitternacht.

Group 2: the half hour

It is one-thirty.
Es ist halb zwei.

It is three-thirty.
Es ist halb vier.

It is five-thirty.
Es ist halb sechs.

It is seven-thirty.
Es ist halb acht.

It is nine-thirty.
Es ist halb zehn.

It is eleven-thirty.
Es ist halb zwölf.

Group 3: quarter of the hour

It is a quarter to two.
Es ist Viertel vor zwei.

It is quarter to four.
Es ist Viertel vor vier.

It is a quarter to six.
Es ist Viertel vor sechs.

It is a quarter to eight.
Es ist Viertel vor acht.

It is quarter to ten.
Es ist Viertel vor zehn.

It is a quarter to twelve.
Es ist Viertel vor zwölf.

Group 4: quarter after the hour

It is quarter after two.
Es ist Viertel nach zwei.

It is quarter after four.
Es ist Viertel nach vier.

It is quarter after six.
Es ist Viertel nach sechs.

It is quarter after eight.
Es ist Viertel nach acht.

It is quarter after ten.
Es ist Viertel nach zehn.

It is quarter after twelve.
Es ist Viertel nach zwölf.

2 Listen to each time expressed in English and then provide the equivalent German expression. *Sag das auf Deutsch!* Repeat each correct answer.

1. at one o'clock
   um ein Uhr
2. at seven-thirty
   um halb acht
3. at quarter to eleven
   um Viertel vor elf
4. at quarter after nine
   um Viertel nach neun
5. at noon
   um Mittag
6. at midnight
   um Mitternacht

3 The next group consists of more precise times. Listen and repeat only the German words.

1. at 7:17
   um siebzehn Minuten nach sieben
2. at 5:12
   um zwölf Minuten nach fünf
3. at 9:35
   um fünfundzwanzig Minuten vor zehn
4. at 2:45
   um Viertel vor drei
5. at 12:50
   um zehn Minuten vor eins

(4) The colors. *Die Farben.* Repeat the following words.

orange / rosa / grau / grün / violett / schwarz / gelb / weiß / braun / blau / rot /

(5) Now let's do a quick check. You will hear a color in English. Say that color in German. *Sag das auf Deutsch!*

1. red / *rot*
2. black / *schwarz*
3. yellow / *gelb*
4. brown / *braun*
5. purple / *violett*
6. blue / *blau*
7. orange / *orange*
8. white / *weiß*
9. gray / *grau*
10. green / *grün*
11. pink / *rosa*

(6) *Welche Farbe hat dieser Vogel?* What color is this bird? In this next activity, you will hear a brief description of a bird. Do you know what color this bird is? If you do, say the color in German. *Sag die Farbe auf Deutsch!*

1. The flamingo is a wading bird with long legs and a strong bill. *Welche Farbe hat dieser Vogel?*
   rosa
2. The wild turkey can fly but it generally looks for food on the ground in woodland areas. *Welche Farbe hat dieser Vogel?*
   braun
3. The common pigeon, or rock dove, is generally seen in city parks. *Welche Farbe hat dieser Vogel?*
   grau
4. The swan has a long neck and lives along the shores of rivers and ponds. *Welche Farbe hat dieser Vogel?*
   weiß
5. The canary is known for its color as well as its voice. *Welche Farbe hat dieser Vogel?*
   gelb
6. This kind of jay has a crest on its head and splashes of white and black. What is its main color? *Welche Farbe hat dieser Vogel?*
   blau
7. The crow is a very large bird known for its distinctive sound, caw. *Welche Farbe hat dieser Vogel?*
   schwarz
8. The bright male cardinal has a crest on its head and a black throat. *Welche Farbe hat dieser Vogel?*
   rot

9. The common parrot may have several colors but its primary one matches the color of the foliage of a tropical rainforest. *Welche Farbe hat dieser Vogel?*
grün
10. One kind of swallow is called the purple martin. *Welche Farbe hat dieser Vogel?*
violett

(7) This is a dictation of ten German words and expressions representing time and colors. Listen carefully, and in the time provided, write them down in your notebook. After you have written each one, you'll hear each word spelled out for you. Correct your work. For capital letters you'll hear "*großes . . .*" For example, you'll hear "*Uhr.*" After writing the word, you'll hear "*großes U, h, r.*"

1. *um drei Uhr*
   That's spelled: *um drei Uhr*
2. *halb*
   That's spelled: *halb*
3. *Wie viel Uhr ist es?*
   That's spelled: *Wie viel Uhr ist es?*
4. *nach*
   That's spelled: *nach*
5. *vor*
   That's spelled: *vor*
6. *die Farben*
   That's spelled: *die Farben*
7. *blau*
   That's spelled: *blau*
8. *rot*
   That's spelled: *rot*
9. *grün*
   That's spelled: *grün*
10. *Welche Farbe hat . . . ?*
    That's spelled: *Welche Farbe hat . . . ?*

Sprichwort

Besser spät als nie.
Wiederhole!
Besser spät / als nie. /

Unit 14

Die Musik
Music

(1) You will hear the names of the famous composers. *Hör zu und wiederhole!*

Johann Sebastian Bach / Wolfgang Amadeus Mozart / Ludwig van Beethoven /

Sprichwort

Das ist Musik in meinen Ohren.
Wiederhole!
Das ist Musik / in meinen Ohren. /

Unit 15

Das Wetter und die Jahreszeiten
Weather and Seasons

1 We will go through the words on page 196 of your book. Listen carefully and repeat them. *Hör zu und wiederhole!*

Wie ist das Wetter? / Es ist schön. / Es ist sonnig. / Es ist warm. / Es ist heiß. / Es ist kühl. / Es ist windig. / Es ist schwül. / Es ist wolkig. / Es ist schlecht. / Es donnert. / Es regnet. / Es blitzt. / Es ist kalt. / Es schneit. /

Welche Jahreszeit haben wir? / die vier Jahreszeiten / der Sommer / der Frühling / der Winter / der Herbst /

2 Let's see if you can remember a few expressions. After you hear each English sentence, say what it means in German. The speaker will provide each answer which you'll repeat. Ready? Let's begin.

1. It's raining.
   Es regnet.
2. It's beautiful.
   Es ist schön.
3. It's cloudy.
   Es ist wolkig.
4. It's thundering.
   Es donnert.
5. It's hot.
   Es ist heiß.
6. It's bad.
   Es ist schlecht.
7. There's lightning.
   Es blitzt.
8. It's humid.
   Es ist schwühl.

3 Complete each sentence by saying how the weather is.

1. Im Sommer ist es . . .
   heiß
2. Im Herbst ist es . . .
   kühl

3. Im Winter ist es . . .
   kalt
4. Im Frühling ist es . . .
   warm

④ Listen now to the dialogues on page 197. *Hör zu!*

MUTTER:	Trage deinen Regenschirm!
KIND:	Warum?
MUTTER:	Es regnet.
MUTTER:	Trage deine Sonnenbrille!
KIND:	Warum?
MUTTER:	Es ist sehr sonnig.
VATER:	Trage deinen Hut!
KIND:	Warum?
VATER:	Es ist sehr kalt.

⑤ After you hear a weather-related word, say what the weather is like or what it is doing. You will then hear an appropriate answer which you will repeat.

1. Sommer
   Es ist heiß.
2. Regenschirm
   Es regnet.
3. Sonnenbrille
   Es ist sonnig.
4. Hut und Handschuhe
   Es ist kalt.
5. Herbst
   Es ist kühl und windig.

⑥ Next you will hear the question: *Welche Jahreszeit haben wir?* followed by an English cue. In the pause provided, answer the question completely by using the German equivalent of that word. Repeat the correct response.

1. Welche Jahreszeit haben wir? *(spring)*
   Wir haben Frühling.
2. Welche Jahreszeit haben wir? *(autumn)*
   Wir haben Herbst.
3. Welche Jahreszeit haben wir? *(summer)*
   Wir haben Sommer.
4. Welche Jahreszeit haben wir? *(winter)*
   Wir haben Winter.

Sprichwort

Morgenstund' hat Gold im Mund.
Wiederhole!
Morgenstund' / hat Gold im Mund. /

Unit 16

Die Tage und die Monate
Days and Months

1 Listen to the short questions and words on page 210 of your textbook. Repeat after the speaker. *Hör zu und wiederhole!*

Welcher Tag ist heute? / Heute ist Montag. / Dienstag / Mittwoch / Donnerstag / Freitag / Samstag / Sonnabend / Sonntag /

Wann ist der Feiertag? / Er ist morgen. / Welches Datum haben wir? / Heute ist der erste August. / der dritte Oktober / der 29. Mai /

Januar / Februar / März / April / Mai / Juni / Juli / August / September / Oktober / November / Dezember /

2 Now you will hear the question again *"Welcher Tag ist heute?"* followed by an English cue. In the time allotted, answer each question completely in German. Repeat each correct answer.

> **Beispiel:** Welcher Tag ist heute? *(Tuesday)*
> Heute ist Dienstag.

1. Welcher Tag ist heute? *(Wednesday)*
   Heute ist Mittwoch.
2. Welcher Tag ist heute? *(Sunday)*
   Heute ist Sonntag.
3. Welcher Tag ist heute? *(Thursday)*
   Heute ist Donnerstag.
4. Welcher Tag ist heute? *(Saturday)*
   Heute ist Samstag.
5. Welcher Tag ist heute? *(Friday)*
   Heute ist Freitag.
6. Welcher Tag ist heute? *(Monday)*
   Heute ist Montag.

3 Let's see now how well you understand the spoken date. You will hear today's date seven different times. After each one, say the date in English. We'll tell you the answer afterwards. *Viel Glück!*

1. *Heute ist der neunte Dezember.*
   Did you say "December 9th?"
   Gut!
2. *Heute ist der dritte Oktober.*
   Did you say "October 3rd?"
   Wunderbar!
3. *Heute ist der siebte November.*
   Did you say "November 7th?"
   Prima!

4. *Heute ist der achtzehnte Juli.*
   Did you say "July 18th?"
   Sehr gut!

5. *Heute ist der erste Januar.*
   Did you say "January 1st?"
   Ausgezeichnet!

6. *Heute ist der dreißigste Juni.*
   Did you say "June 30th?"
   Sehr gut!

7. *Heute ist der vierundzwanzigste April.*
   Did you say "April 24th?"
   Prima!

(4) Katja has a vocabulary list to study. Listen to her list and say each word afterwards. *Hör zu und wiederhole!*

morgen / übermorgen / gestern / vorgestern / der Tag / der Feiertag / der Schultag / der Geburtstag / die Woche / das Wochenende / der Monat / heute /

Now Katja will say them in English, and you can say them in German. Listen afterwards for the correct answer.

the week / *die Woche*
the month / *der Monat*
the weekend / *das Wochenende*
the holiday / *der Feiertag*
the day / *der Tag*
the birthday / *der Geburtstag*
the school day / *der Schultag*
tomorrow / *morgen*
the day after tomorrow / *übermorgen*
yesterday / *gestern*
the day before yesterday / *vorgestern*
today / *heute*

(5) Listen to the dialogues about the days of the week and dates. *Hör zu!*

TIM:	Wann hast du Geburtstag, Jens?
JENS:	Er ist übermorgen, am achten Juni.
MAJA:	An welchem Tag ist die Englischarbeit?
MICHAEL:	Sie ist am Dienstag.
LAURA:	Was hast du heute, Andreas?
ANDREAS:	Ich habe gar nichts. Heute habe ich frei.
BETTINA:	Was hast du am Mittwoch?
NATASCHA:	Ich habe meine Klavierstunde.

6 Now give short answers in German, this time using the English cues. Repeat the correct answers.

1. Wann hast du Geburtstag? *(tomorrow, on November 15ᵗʰ)*
Morgen, am fünfzehnten November.
2. An welchem Tag ist die Deutscharbeit? *(on Monday)*
Am Montag.
3. Was hast du am Mittwoch? *(my piano lesson)*
Meine Klavierstunde.
4. Was hast du heute? *(nothing at all)*
Gar nichts!

Sprichwort

Morgen, morgen, nur nicht heute, sagen alle faulen Leute.
Wiederhole!
Morgen, morgen, / nur nicht heute, / sagen alle faulen Leute. /

Unit 17

Die Literatur
Literature

1 Repeat the names of the authors, cities, and literary works presented in this unit.

Johann Wolfgang von Goethe / Frankfurt / Faust / Iphigenie auf Tauris / Wilhelm Meister / Die Leiden des jungen Werthers / Friedrich Schiller / Marbach / Mannheim / Maria Stuart / Wilhelm Tell / An die Freude / Ernst Theodor Amadeus Hoffmann / Königsberg / Nachtstücke / Nussknacker und Mausekönig / Else Lasker-Schüler / Berlin / Styx / Der siebente Tag / Hebräische Balladen / Christa Wolf / Landsberg / Der geteilte Himmel / Nachdenken über Christa T / Kassandra / Sarah Kirsch / Die Deutsche Demokratische Republik / Die Pantherfrau / Landaufenthalt / Zaubersprüche /

2 Can you name the literary work? You will hear a clue for each work. In the pause provided guess the name of the literary work.

1. This play is set in the days when the Swiss people were struggling to stay independent.
Wilhelm Tell
2. This poem is about the simple things in everyday life, for example lilac trees and gardens.
Landaufenthalt
3. This story is like a fairy tale; the characters in a dream come alive.
Nussknacker und Mausekönig
4. This play is about a transaction made between a human being and a devil.
Faust
5. This poetry is about love, friendship, and loss.
Styx
6. This story is about a boy and a girl whose lives are disrupted by political differences.
Der geteilte Himmel

Sprichwort

Wer A sagt, muss auch B sagen.
Wiederhole!
Wer A sagt, / muss auch B sagen. /

Unit 18

Die Freizeit
Leisure and Recreation

1 Now let's see how many phrases you remember. After you hear the question *"Wohin gehst du?"* answer it by using the cue. Repeat each answer after the speaker.

> **Beispiel:** You hear: Wohin gehst du? (zum Fußballspiel)
> You say: Ich gehe zum Fußballspiel.

1. Wohin gehst du? (ins Museum)
   Ich gehe ins Museum.

2. Wohin gehst du? (auf die Party)
   Ich gehe auf die Party.

3. Wohin gehst du? (zum Strand)
   Ich gehe zum Strand.

2 After you hear the question *"Welche Sportart treibst du?"* use the cue to give your answer. Repeat each answer after the speaker.

> **Beispiel:** You hear: Welche Sportart treibst du? (Baseball)
> You say: Ich spiele Baseball.

1. Welche Sportart treibst du? (Volleyball)
   Ich spiele Volleyball.

2. Welche Sportart treibst du? (Basketball)
   Ich spiele Basketball.

3. Welche Sportart treibst du? (Fußball)
   Ich spiele Fußball.

4. Welche Sportart treibst du? (Tennis)
   Ich spiele Tennis.

3 The next question is *"Was machst du gern?"* The cue will be in English. Use the cue to answer the question in German. Repeat each correct response.

> **Beispiel:** You hear: Was machst du gern? *(ski)*
> You reply: Ich laufe gern Ski.

1. Was machst du gern? *(read)*
   Ich lese gern.

2. Was machst du gern? *(horseback ride)*
   Ich reite gern.

3. Was machst du gern? *(dance)*
   Ich tanze gern.

4. Was machst du gern? *(swim)*
   Ich schwimme gern.

5. Was machst du gern? *(ride a bike)*
   Ich fahre gern Rad.

6. Was machst du gern? *(play football)*
   Ich spiele gern amerikanischen Fußball.

(4) In this next activity you will hear clues in English. Say a related German noun for each one. Listen first to the example.

> **Beispiel:** You hear: swimming
> You say: *der Strand*

1. famous paintings
   das Museum
2. balloons and cake
   die Party
3. soccer game
   das Fußballspiel
4. songs and CDs
   die Musik
5. racket and ball
   das Tennis
6. outdoor lunch
   das Picknick

(5) Now let's say there are three activities that you do not like to do. Use the English cue.

> **Beispiel:** Say that you do not like to swim.
> You say: *Ich schwimme nicht gern.*

1. Say that you do not like to horseback ride.
   Ich reite nicht gern.

2. Say that you do not like to ski.
   Ich laufe nicht gern Ski.

3. Say that you do not like to play volleyball.
   Ich spiele nicht gern Volleyball.

(6) Now you can evaluate your own interests. You will hear 12 questions which ask whether or not you enjoy doing a certain activity. Answer each one with either *ja* or *nein*, depending on your personal preferences.

1. Schwimmst du gern?
2. Tanzt du gern?
3. Liest du gern?
4. Läufst du gern Ski?
5. Spielst du gern Baseball?
6. Spielst du gern Fußball?
7. Reitest du gern?
8. Fährst du gern Rad?
9. Hörst du gern Musik?
10. Arbeitest du gern im Garten?
11. Zeichnest du gern?
12. Sprichst du gern deutsch?

(7) Listen to the the reading passage on page 242 of your textbook. *Hör zu!*

Thomas hat heute eine Geburtstagsparty am Strand. Heute ist er vierzehn Jahre alt. Das Wetter ist warm und schön. Die Party beginnt um drei Uhr. Wer kommt zur Party? Sieben Freunde. Sie sind glücklich. Sie spielen Volleyball, schwimmen und tanzen. Es gibt viel zu essen und trinken: Butterbrote, Eis und natürlich einen Geburtstagskuchen. Ein Picknick am Strand ist eine prima Idee!

Sprichwort

In der Abwechslung liegt das Vergnügen.
Wiederhole!
In der Abwechslung / liegt das Vergnügen. /

Unit 19

Das Einkaufen
Shopping

(1) In this unit you'll learn some basic words and expressions about shopping. First listen and repeat the words and phrases. Then listen to the dialogues on page 250.

Ich kaufe . . . ein. / im Einkaufszentrum / die Kundin / der Verkäufer / die Tennisschuhe /

Now listen to the following dialogues. *Hör zu!*

| VERKÄUFER: | Guten Morgen! Was darf es sein? |
| KUNDIN: | Nein, danke. Ich schaue mich nur um. |

VERKÄUFER:	Guten Morgen! Was darf es sein?
KUNDIN:	Ja, bitte. Ich möchte ein Buch kaufen.
VERKÄUFER:	Gut. Unsere Auswahl is sehr groß.

RUTH:	Wohin gehst du?
RÜDIGER:	Zum Einkaufszentrum.
RUTH:	Was kaufst du dort?
RÜDIGER:	Tennisschuhe.

Now listen and repeat some more words and then listen to two more dialogues on page 251.

im Geschäft / die Kasse / das Kleingeld / das Geld / die Kassiererin / der Kunde / das Angebot / die Compact Disc / die CD / auf dem Markt / die Pfirsiche / die grünen Bohnen / die Verkäuferin /

Listen to two more dialogues. *Hör zu!*

KUNDE:	Wie viel kostet diese CD?
KASSIERERIN:	Sie kostet € 12.
KUNDE:	Das ist etwas teuer!
KASSIERERIN:	Nein, das ist billig.
KUNDE:	Also, gut. Ich kaufe die CD. Hier ist das Geld.
KASSIERERIN:	Danke schön. Da ist Ihr Kleingeld.

| VERKÄUFERIN: | Noch etwas? |
| KUNDE: | Ja, drei Tomaten, fünf Pfirsiche und grüne Bohnen. Das ist alles. |

2 Check your memory now and see if you remember a few words and phrases. After you hear an English word, say it in German. You will hear the correct answer afterwards.

1. shopping
   das Einkaufen
2. at the shopping center
   im Einkaufszentrum
3. at the store
   im Geschäft
4. at the market
   auf dem Markt
5. to buy
   kaufen
6. to shop
   einkaufen
7. to cost
   kosten
8. our selection
   unsere Auswahl
9. expensive
   teuer
10. cheap, inexpensive
    billig

3 Now do five sentence completions based on the dialogues in this unit. First you will hear an English sentence, followed by part of its German equivalent. Finish the sentence by adding the remaining word.

> **Beispiel:** You hear: Good morning! May I help you? *Guten Morgen! Was darf es . . . ?*
> You reply: *sein*

1. Where are you going? *Wohin gehst . . . ?*
   du
2. To the shopping center. *Zum . . .*
   Einkaufszentrum
3. What are you going to buy there? *Was kaufst du . . . ?*
   dort
4. I'd like to buy a book. *Ich möchte ein Buch . . .*
   kaufen
5. Our selection is very large. *Unsere Auswahl ist sehr . . .*
   groß

4 Ask about how much the following items cost by saying, *"Wie viel kostet?"* Pay attention to the article before the noun. Repeat each question.

> **Beispiele:** der Mantel
> Wie viel kostet der Mantel?
>
> eine Bluse
> Wie viel kostet eine Bluse?

1. der Computer
   Wie viel kostet der Computer?
2. ein Buch
   Wie viel kostet ein Buch?
3. das Haus
   Wie viel kostet das Haus?
4. ein Pfirsich
   Wie viel kostet ein Pfirsich?
5. die Lampe
   Wie viel kostet die Lampe?
6. eine CD
   Wie viel kostet eine CD?

5 You are the salesclerk today. Answer each customer's question about the price of an item. Say the suggested price in German. Repeat each answer.

> **Beispiel:** You hear: Wie viel kostet der Fußball? (30 Euro)
> You say: Der Fußball kostet dreißig Euro.

1. Wie viel kostet der Rock? (49 Euro)
   Der Rock kostet 49 Euro.

2. Wie viel kostet der Anzug? (120 Euro)
   Der Anzug kostet 120 Euro.
3. Wie viel kostet die DVD? (15 Euro)
   Die DVD kostet 15 Euro.
4. Wie viel kostet das Fahrrad? (200 Euro)
   Das Fahrrad kostet 200 Euro.
5. Wie viel kostet das Eis? (1,50 Euro)
   Das Eis kostet 1,50 Euro.

(6) Now the customers are asking about the price of several items. Listen to the model and answer each question using the price given. Repeat each correct response.

> **Beispiel:** You hear: Wie viel kosten die CDs? (10 Euros)
> You answer: Die CDs kosten zehn Euro.

1. Wie viel kosten die Tomaten? (1,20 Euros)
   Die Tomaten kosten 1,20 Euro.
2. Wie viel kosten die Pfirsiche? (3 Euros)
   Die Pfirsiche kosten 3 Euro.
3. Wie viel kosten die Jacken? (39 Euros)
   Die Jacken kosten 39 Euro.
4. Wie viel kosten die Hemden? (20 Euros)
   Die Hemden kosten 20 Euro.

(7) You will now hear a short dictation of six sentences in German. Each will be read twice. In the allotted time write each sentence in your notebook. Are you ready? *Hör zu und schreib!*

1. Das ist teuer.
2. Das ist billig.
3. Hier ist das Geld.
4. Da ist Ihr Kleingeld.
5. Noch etwas?
6. Das ist alles.

Sprichwort

Wer den Pfennig nicht ehrt, ist des Talers nicht wert.
Wiederhole!
Wer den Pfennig / nicht ehrt, / ist des Talers nicht wert. /

Unit 20

Das Reisen und der Verkehr
Travel and Transportation

(1) Listen to the following sentences and repeat them. *Hör zu und wiederhole!*

> Wie reist du? / Ich reise mit dem Flugzeug. / Ich fahre mit dem Auto. / Ich fahre mit dem Schiff. / Ich fahre mit dem Bus. / Ich fahre mit dem Zug. / Ich fliege. /

(2) Let's check those new words. After you hear an English cue, say it in German. You will hear the correct words immediately afterwards, which you will repeat.

1. by ship
   mit dem Schiff
2. by car
   mit dem Auto
3. by bus
   mit dem Bus
4. by airplane
   mit dem Flugzug
5. by train
   mit dem Zug
6. I travel by car.
   Ich fahre mit dem Auto.
7. I travel by train.
   Ich fahre mit dem Zug.
8. I travel by ship.
   Ich fahre mit dem Schiff.
9. I travel by bus.
   Ich fahre mit dem Bus.
10. I travel by plane.
    Ich reise mit dem Flugzeug.

(3) The check-in counter at the airport is our next stop. Listen and repeat the list of words useful at the airport. Then listen to a short conversation between a female airline clerk and a male traveler.

> auf dem Flughafen / die Angestellte / der Reisende / der Reisepass / der Schalter / der Koffer/

Now listen to the conversation. *Hör zu!*

ANGESTELLTE:	Ihren Reisepass, bitte?
REISENDER:	Er ist in meinem Koffer.
ANGESTELLTE:	Sie brauchen ihn, wenn Sie bei der Passkontrolle ankommen.
REISENDER:	Also, gut. Warten Sie, bitte! . . . Hier ist mein Reisepass. Wo steht das Flugzeug?
ANGESTELLTE:	Am Flugsteig 20. Dort drüben, rechts. Gute Reise!

(4) This section is a review of some airport words and phrases. After you hear an English phrase, say it in German. You will hear the correct words which you will repeat.

1. at the airport
   auf dem Flughafen
2. the suitcase
   der Koffer
3. the female clerk or employee
   die Angestellte
4. the passport
   der Reisepass
5. the male traveler
   der Reisende
6. the ticket counter
   der Schalter

(5) From the airport we go to the train station, where we have some more words and phrases. *Hör zu und wiederhole!*

der Angestellte / die Fahrkarte / die Reisende / der Fahrplan / auf dem Bahnhof /

At the train station we find a woman asking for information. *Hör zu!*

REISENDE:	Um wie viel Uhr fährt der nächste Zug nach Berlin?
ANGESTELLTER:	Um zwölf Uhr. Hier ist der Fahrplan.
REISENDE:	Danke. Ich möchte eine Rückfahrkarte, zweite Klasse.
ANGESTELLTER:	Hier ist Ihre Fahrkarte. Das macht € 120.

(6) We go now to a bus stop along a city street. Frau Schubert, who is waiting for her bus, helps out another traveler, Herr Mendelssohn. *Hör zu!*

HERR MENDELSSOHN:	Enschuldigen Sie! Wie komme ich zum Hotel Krone?
FRAU SCHUBERT:	Fahren Sie mit dem Bus Nummer 2 und steigen Sie am Park aus! Das Hotel ist links.

Now answer a couple of questions in German.

1. Wo ist Herr Mendelssohn?
   Auf der Straße.
2. Wie reist er zum Hotel Krone?
   Mit dem Bus.

(7) Now you will be asked to say the conversation in German. After you hear a line of the dialogue in English, provide the German equivalent.

1. Excuse me.
   Entschuldigen Sie!
2. How do I get to Hotel Krone?
   Wie komme ich zum Hotel Krone?

3. Take bus number 2.
   Fahren Sie mit Bus Nummer zwei!
4. Get off at the park.
   Steigen Sie am Park aus!
5. The hotel is on the left.
   Das Hotel ist links.

Sprichwort

Das Reisen bildet.
Wiederhole!
Das Reisen / bildet. /

Check-up Written Activities

Unit 1

A Tell whether the names listed below are for a girl or a boy. Write *Mädchen* or *Junge* next to the name. (6 points)

1. Eberhard _____
2. Petra _____
3. Sabine _____
4. Günther _____
5. Beate _____
6. Jochen _____

B Write the following words in German. (4 points)

1. English _____
2. German _____
3. please _____
4. good-bye _____

C Match the situation with the German responses. (10 points)

Situations

1. _____ It's bedtime now. What do you say to your family?
2. _____ Your friend is going ice skating for the first time. How do you express your hope that she will be successful?
3. _____ You accidentally bump into someone on the school playground. How do you excuse yourself?
4. _____ One afternoon you see your neighbor, Mr. Müller, in front of his house. How do you say hello to him?
5. _____ When you see your friend, Benjamin, how do you greet him?
6. _____ How do you answer the question *Wie heißt du?*
7. _____ You feel bad because you hurt someone's feelings. What do you say to that person?
8. _____ Someone asks you whether you speak Chinese. Say you do.
9. _____ The same person asks you whether you speak Russian. Say you don't.
10. _____ Your friend has been ill. Ask him how he is today.

Responses

A. Ich heiße . . . (name).

B. Ich spreche chinesisch.

C. Tag!

D. Wie geht's?

E. Es tut mir leid.

F. Gute Nacht!

G. Entschuldigung!

H. Ich spreche nicht russisch.

I. Guten Tag!

J. Viel Glück!

Unit 2

A Complete each sentence by writing in the missing words using the English clues. (10 points)

1. Was ist _____? (that)

2. Das ist _____ Tafel. (a)

3. Das ist _____ Fenster. (a)

4. Das ist _____ Fahne. (a)

5. Das ist _____ Computer. (a)

6. Das ist ein _____. (notebook)

7. Das ist eine _____. (class)

8. Das ist ein _____. (pen)

9. Das ist ein Blatt _____. (paper)

10. Das ist ein _____. (ruler)

B Finish each classroom command by circling the letter of the correct word(s). (5 points)

1. Mach . . . auf!
   A. das Buch
   B. die Frage
   C. das Bild

2. Beantworte die . . . !
   A. Sätze
   B. Frage
   C. Uhr

3. Nimm . . . !
   A. auf Deutsch
   B. ein Klassenzimmer
   C. ein Blatt Papier heraus

4. Geh . . . !
   A. an die Sätze
   B. an die Hand
   C. an die Tafel

5. Ergänze . . . !
   A. die Uhr
   B. die Sätze
   C. die Fahne

C **Circle the letter of the object which relates to the classroom command. (5 points)**

1. Schreib!
   A. ein Bild
   B. ein Kuli

2. Heb!
   A. die Hand
   B. Computer

3. Lies!
   A. das Buch
   B. das Lineal

4. Wiederhole!
   A. das Lineal
   B. die Frage

5. Schalte an!
   A. deutsch
   B. Computer

Unit 3

 A **Write Arabic numerals. For each number you see below, make its corresponding Arabic numeral. (5 points)**

> **Beispiel:**   fünf: <u>5</u>

1. neun: _____

2. einundzwanzig: _____

3. achtundsechzig: _____

4. dreiunddreißig: _____

5. achtzig: _____

B **Circle the correct answer. (5 points)**

1. Vier mal neun ist . . .
   A. dreizehn
   B. sechsunddreißig
   C. neunzig

2. Fünfundsiebzig weniger sechzig ist . . .
   A. einundzwanzig
   B. fünfzehn
   C. elf

3. Eins und sieben ist . . .
   A. acht
   B. einundsiebzig
   C. siebzehn

4. Zwei mal sechs ist . . .
   A. vierzehn
   B. zweiunddreißig
   C. zwölf

5. Achtzig geteilt durch zwei ist . . .
   A. acht
   B. zehn
   C. vierzig

C *Beantworte die Fragen!* **Read each question and then answer by writing a complete sentence in German. (5 points)**

1. Wie viel kostet ein Buch?

   _____

2. Wie viel kostet ein Stuhl?

   _____

3. Wie viel kosten zwei Kulis?

   _____

4. Wie viele Computer gibt es?

   _____

5. Wie viele Fenster gibt es?

   _____

D **Numerical Sequences. Figure out the sequence of numbers. Fill in the missing number in each sequence. Write it in German (5 points)**

1. sieben, _____, neun

2. zehn, fünfzehn, _____

3. null, eins, _____

4. vierzig, _____, achtzig

5. dreiunddreißig, _____, neununddreißig

Unit 4

 Geography. Write a short answer to each question. (10 points)

1. Is the *Main* a mountain range or a river?

   _____

2. Is Italy one of Switzerland's neighbors?

   _____

3. Does France lie to the southeast or the southwest of Germany?

   _____

4. Is the *Harz* a mountain range or a river?

   _____

5. What happens frequently in the Alps during spring thaws?

   _____

6. In which direction does the Danube River flow?

   _____

7. What is the English name of *die Ostsee*?

   _____

8. What is the English name of *Österreich*?

   _____

9. Where are Germany's lowlands: north or south?

   _____

10. Between what two countries is the principality of Liechtenstein?

   _____

B **Which German city relates to which fact? (5 points)**

City		Facts
1. _____	München	A. birthplace of the poet and statesman Goethe
2. _____	Frankfurt	B. site of the Brandenburg Gate
3. _____	Berlin	C. site of many parks and waterways
4. _____	Köln	D. southern city with an Olympic stadium
5. _____	Hamburg	E. city started as a Roman colony

C **Which Austrian or Swiss city relates to which fact? (5 points)**

City		Facts
1. _____	Salzburg	A. birthplace of the composer Mozart
2. _____	Zürich	B. lake city and conference center
3. _____	Bern	C. banking and financial center
4. _____	Wien (Vienna)	D. capital city of Switzerland
5. _____	Genf (Geneva)	E. capital city and river port

Unit 5

A Write the following words in German. Remember to write the definite article, *der*, *die*, or *das* first. (5 points)

1. the house _____

2. the yard or garden _____

3. the living room _____

4. the patio _____

5. the kitchen _____

B Complete the sentences below by choosing the correct words from the list. (5 points)

> WO
> Schlafzimmer
> hinter
> Ich wohne
> Mietshaus

1. Es gibt viele Wohnungen in dem _____.

2. _____ in Zürich.

3. Die Garage ist _____ dem Garten.

4. _____ ist die Wohnung?

5. Das _____ ist schön.

C Match the descriptions with the places. (5 points)

A	B
1. _____ the room where you would eat a special dinner	A. die Hütte
2. _____ the place where flowers grow	B. das Esszimmer
3. _____ the room to bathe	C. die Villa
4. _____ small simple shelter	D. der Garten
5. _____ very large house	E. das Badezimmer

D Write in the missing German words using the English clues. (5 points)

1. Wo _____ du? *(do you live)*

2. Das _____ ist sehr schön. *(tent)*

3. Es gibt sechs _____. *(rooms)*

4. Ich wohne nicht in einer _____. *(mansion)*

5. Das ist ein _____. *(single family house)*

Unit

A Write the opposite of each word listed. (6 points)

> **Beispiel:** die Mutter
> der Vater

1. die Schwester _____

2. der Pate _____

3. der Cousin _____

4. die Enkelin _____

5. der Mann _____

6. der Sohn _____

B Choose the correct answer. (4 points)

1. Wer ist das?
   A. Das ist meine Schwester, Tanja.
   B. Meine Schwester, Tanja, ist auf der Terrasse.

2. Wer sind die Kinder?
   A. Die Kinder sind in dem Garten.
   B. Die Kinder sind meine Cousins.

3. Sind Anna und Tim deine Verwandten?
   A. Das Familientreffen.
   B. Ja.

4. Wo sind deine Eltern?
   A. In dem Wohnzimmer.
   B. Mein Vater und meine Mutter.

C Read the following passage and circle the best answer for each question that follows. (10 points)

Das Familientreffen von Kahns ist in dem Haus von Samuels Großeltern. Die Kinder sind im Garten. Die Schwester von Samuel, Julia, spricht mit ihrer Kusine, Sophie. Auf der Terrasse spricht Onkel Andreas mit *seinem* Bruder, Johann und Tante Katja ist da mit Raimund, dem Großvater von Samuel. Frau Fischer ist drinnen. Sie *bewundert* Monikas Baby. In dem Wohnzimmer sind *auch* die Eltern von Samuel und Julia: Martin und Claudia, und *andere Erwachsene. Im Ganzen* gibt es zwölf Erwachsene, sieben Kinder und ein Baby.

seinem	his	**andere Erwachsene**	other adults
bewundert	admires	**Im Ganzen**	altogether
auch	also		

1. Wo sind die Kinder?
   A. Samuel und Sophie.
   B. Sieben Kinder.
   C. Im Garten.

2. Wer ist Julia?
   A. Die Tante von Samuel.
   B. Die Schwester von Samuel.
   C. Die Kusine von Samuel.

3. Wie heißt die Kusine von Julia?
   A. Claudia.
   B. Monika.
   C. Sophie.

4. Wer spricht mit Johann?
   A. Onkel Andreas.
   B. Frau Fischer.
   C. Das Baby.

5. Wie heißt der Großvater von Samuel?
   A. Martin.
   B. Raimund.
   C. Andreas.

6. Wo ist Frau Fischer?
   A. In dem Haus.
   B. In dem Garten.
   C. Auf der Terrasse.

7. Wer hat (has) ein Baby?
   A. Sophie.
   B. Monika.
   C. Claudia.

8. Wer sind Martin und Claudia?
   A. Der Onkel und die Tante von Samuel und Julia.
   B. Der Vater und die Mutter von Samuel und Julia.
   C. Der Bruder und die Schwester von Samuel und Julia.

9. Wo gibt es viele Erwachsene?
   A. Im Garten.
   B. Im Esszimmer.
   C. Im Wohnzimmer.

10. Wie viele Personen gibt es im Ganzen?
    A. Zwanzig.
    B. Zwölf.
    C. Sieben.

Unit 7

A Identify each animal by writing its German name. Start with the words *Das ist* and be sure to include the indefinite article *ein* or *eine*. (5 points)

1. _____

2. _____

3. _____

4. _____

5. _____

B Write the missing German words using the English cues. (5 points)

1. Die Kinder sind auf dem _____. *(country)*

2. Die Enten sind auf dem _____. *(pond)*

3. Die Tiere sind im _____. *(stall, stable)*

4. Die Kühe sind auf der _____. *(pasture)*

5. Die Vögel sind in der _____. *(air)*

C Circle the correct response to each German question or statement. (10 points)

1. Was ist das?
   A. Das ist ein Schwein.
   B. Das ist ein Junge.

2. Was machst du?
   A. Ich sammle die Eier.
   B. Es gibt viele Eier.

3. Wer ist das?
   A. Das ist ein Eimer.
   B. Das ist Simon.

4. Wie heißt das Mädchen?
   A. Jutta.
   B. Simon.

5. Wie ist die Ente?
   A. Die Ente ist groß.
   B. Die Ente ist klein.

6. Wie sind die Schweine?
   A. Die Schweine sind groß.
   B. Die Schweine sind klein.

7. Wo ist der Esel?
   A. Der Esel ist im Stall.
   B. Der Esel ist in der Luft.

8. Komm mit! Ich füttre jetzt die Tiere.
   A. Das ist eine Ziege.
   B. Schön. Ich möchte helfen.

9. Gibt es auch Hennen?
   A. Die Kühe sind groß.
   B. Ja. Sie sind hinter der Scheune.

10. Ich möchte helfen.
    A. Ja, sicher! Du kannst den Eimer halten.
    B. Es gibt viele Tiere.

Unit 8

A Complete each sentence in German with the name of the occupation indicated in English in the parentheses. (8 points)

1. Daniel ist _____. *(cook)*

2. Johanna ist _____. *(musician)*

3. Niklas ist _____. *(letter carrier)*

4. Diana ist _____. *(businesswoman)*

5. Frau Meier _____. *(nurse)*

6. Herr Hofer ist _____. *(computer programmer)*

7. Mein Onkel Michael ist _____. *(carpenter)*

8. Meine Tante Antje ist _____. *(electrician)*

B Using the sentence as a cue, identify the occupation of the person. Start your answer with *Ich bin*. The *(m.)* or *(f.)* indicates whether you should write the word for a male or a female person. (5 points)

1. Ich arbeite auf dem Lande. *(m.)* _____

2. Ich arbeite in einem Theater. *(f.)* _____

3. Ich arbeite in einem Restaurant. *(m.)* _____

4. Ich arbeite mit Computern. *(f.)* _____

5. Ich arbeite mit Mädchen und Jungen in der Schule. *(m.)* _____

C Read each question and then answer it with a complete sentence in German. (Hint: How would each person answer the question?) Use the English cue in parentheses to form your answer. (4 points)

1. Cornelia, was ist dein Beruf? *(physician)*

   _____

2. Paul, was machst du? *(mechanic)*

   _____

D **Read the following questions and circle the letter of the best response. (3 points)**

1. Arbeitest du gern?
   A. Ja.
   B. Zwei.
   C. Elektriker.

2. Wo arbeitest du?
   A. Drei Klempner.
   B. Ich bin Landwirt.
   C. Im Theater.

3. Was ist Alex?
   A. Köchin.
   B. Schauspieler.
   C. Beruf.

Unit 9

A Write an answer in German to each question. (6 points)

1. Hast du Durst?

   _____

2. Hast du Hunger?

   _____

3. Was gibt es zu essen?

   _____

4. Was gibt es zu trinken?

   _____

5. Was isst du?

   _____

6. Was trinkst du?

   _____

B Circle the letter that correctly completes the sentence or answers the question. (14 points)

1. *Tomatensaft* is . . .
   A. a beverage
   B. a vegetable
   C. a soup

2. *Das Abendessen* is . . .
   A. mid-day meal
   B. light evening meal
   C. breakfast

3. *Das Eis* is . . .
   A. an appetizer
   B. a dessert
   C. a main dish

4. *Schweinebraten* is . . .
   A. roast pork
   B. buttered noodles
   C. melted cheese

5. *Lebkuchen* consists of . . .
   A. candied fruits and nuts
   B. honey and spices
   C. cream filling and strawberries

6. A *Birne* is . . .
   A. a pear
   B. a pineapple
   C. a banana

7. *Brot* is . . .
   A. banana
   B. chicken broth
   C. bread

8. *Lebensmittel* refers to . . .
   A. fresh fruit
   B. groceries
   C. desserts

9. *Eberhards Ecke* is a . . .
   A. restaurant with regional food
   B. fast-food diner
   C. first class restaurant

10. A sign reads *Getränke*. What is being sold?
    A. frozen food
    B. canned food
    C. beverages

11. What kind of meal is this: *Tomatensuppe, Hühnerfrikassee, grüne Bohnen, Kartoffeln, gemischter Salat und Obst*?
    A. light supper
    B. breakfast
    C. traditional midday meal

12. What do you need to stir your chocolate milk?
    A. *Löffel*
    B. *Messer*
    C. *Gabel*

13. This word means thirst:
    A. *Milch*
    B. *Durst*
    C. *Teller*

14. *Guten Appetit!* means something like:
    A. May you enjoy the meal!
    B. Hope you can stay for dessert!
    C. Please give my compliments to the cook!

Unit

A **The Art. Choose one of the paintings or works of art listed below and complete the information about it. (5 points)**

A. *The Young Hare*
B. *Saint Anthony*
C. *The Large Blue Horses*
D. *Women in the Street, Berlin*
E. *Ships in the Harbor of Greifswald*
F. *Lone Tree*

Your selection: _____

1. Who or what is in the picture?

_____

2. The artist is . . .

_____

3. The major colors are . . .

_____

4. Why I like it . . .

_____

5. Why I don't like it . . .

_____

B **The Styles. Write the name of the art style (Classicism, Romanticism, Expressionism) in the space provided. (3 points)**

1. heavy dark outlines, bright colors, primitive features

_____

2. clear, natural and proportional lines

_____

3. fairly realistic but conveying feeling or mood

_____

C **The Artists.** *Wer ist das?* Who is this? Decide which artist in Unit 10 fits each description. Write the name in the space provided. Choose from: Dürer, Friedrich, Kirchner, Dietz, Votteler, Richter, and Marc. One name will be used more than once. (8 points)

This artist . . .

1. enjoyed making landscapes and seascapes

_____

2. makes etchings of birds, flowers, and children

_____

3. started an art movement called the "Bridge"

_____

4. uses art to help protect natural resources

_____

5. created fine, realistic drawings, and wood cuts

_____

6. combines photography and painting

_____

7. was a member of the "Blue Rider" group

_____

8. signed his work with his initials

_____

D **Match the names of the artists with their creations. (4 points)**

1. _____ Gerhard Richter   A. sculptures

2. _____ Neo Rauch and Matthias Weischer   B. paintings showing new and old techniques

3. _____ Jutta Votteler   C. "blurry" paintings

4. _____ Madeleine Dietz   D. etchings

Unit 11

A Write the German words for these parts of the body. (8 points)

1. the nose   _____
2. the ear   _____
3. the eye   _____
4. the mouth   _____
5. the leg   _____
6. the forehead   _____
7. the foot   _____
8. the elbow   _____

B Give the English equivalents of the following sentences. (4 points)

1. Ich bin krank.   _____
2. Benjamin ist traurig.   _____
3. Du bist glücklich.   _____
4. Ich habe Kopfweh.   _____

C Beantworte die Fragen auf Deutsch! *(Answer each question in a complete German sentence.)* (8 points)

1. Wie fühlst du dich?

   _____

2. Wie geht's?

   _____

3. Bist du traurig?

   _____

4. Ist Rainer krank?

   _____

Unit 12

A Write the German words for these articles of clothing. (5 points)

1. the blouse   _____
2. the belt   _____
3. the bathrobe   _____
4. the handkerchief   _____
5. the pants, trousers   _____

B Write an answer to each question in German. The cue tells you where the clothing would be appropriate. (6 points)

1. Was hast du an? (Konzert)

_____

2. Was hast du an? (Garten)

_____

3. Wie ist der Schlafanzug?

_____

C Which item of clothing can be worn with a . . .? Circle the best answer. (5 points)

1. Rock
   A. Bluse
   B. Mütze

2. Mantel
   A. Socken
   B. Hut

3. Hose
   A. Gürtel
   B. Kleid

4. Schlafanzug
   A. Bademantel
   B. Schuhe

5. Krawatte
   A. Taschentuch
   B. Hemd

D Answer each question by choosing the correct letter of the corresponding answer. (4 points)

A	B
1. _____ Which sentence tells you how something is or what it is like?	A. Ich packe meinen Koffer.
2. _____ Which sentence tells you where I am going?	B. Ich reise bald in die Schweiz.
3. _____ Which sentence tells you what I'm doing?	C. Ich habe einen Skianzug.
4. _____ Which sentence tells you what I have?	D. Mein Kleid ist schön.

Unit 13

A **Identify the following times of day. Write your answer in the space provided. (5 points)**

1. Es ist ein Uhr.   _____

2. Es ist Viertel vor neun.   _____

3. Es ist sieben Uhr zehn.   _____

4. Es ist zwanzig vor drei.   _____

5. Es ist halb elf.   _____

B **Express the following times using the space provided. (3 points)**

1. Es ist Mitternacht.   _____.

2. Es ist Mittag.   _____.

3. Um wie viel Uhr?   _____.

C **Beantworte die Fragen!** *(Write out complete sentences in German.)* **(4 points)**

1. Um wie viel Uhr ist die Party?

   _____

2. Wie viel Uhr ist es?

   _____

3. Welche Farbe hat der Hund?

   _____

4. Welche Farbe haben die Tomaten?

   _____

D Circle the letter of the correct completion. (4 points)

1. Die Banane ist . . .
   A. gelb
   B. blau

2. Die Rose ist . . .
   A. braun
   B. rot

3. Die Tiger sind . . .
   A. rot und braun
   B. orange und schwarz

4. Das Gras ist . . .
   A. grün
   B. violett

E Write the German equivalents of the following colors in the space provided. (4 points)

1. color _____

2. time _____

3. gray _____

4. pink _____

Unit 14

A **Identify each of the following people. Choose from: Beethoven, Quasthoff, Mozart, and Bach. (4 points)**

1. Baroque musician

   _____

2. Romantic musician

   _____

3. Classical musician

   _____

4. singer of classical songs

   _____

B **Circle the correct answer. (10 points)**

1. He worked in Leipzig.
   A. Bach
   B. Beethoven
   C. Mozart

2. He came from Bonn.
   A. Bach
   B. Beethoven
   C. Mozart

3. He wrote music for the organ, keyboard, and harpsichord.
   A. Bach
   B. Beethoven
   C. Mozart

4. He valued the ideals of freedom and equality.
   A. Bach
   B. Mozart
   C. Beethoven

5. He directed a church choir.
   A. Beethoven
   B. Bach
   C. Mozart

6. He wrote *The Brandenburg Concertos*.
   A. Mozart
   B. Beethoven
   C. Bach

7. He created the *Moonlight Sonata* and the opera *Fidelio*.
   A. Bach
   B. Beethoven
   C. Mozart

8. He wrote *Eine kleine Nachtmusik*.
   A. Mozart
   B. Beethoven
   C. Bach

9. He earned very little money in spite of his talent.
   A. Bach
   B. Beethoven
   C. Mozart

10. He became deaf.
    A. Bach
    B. Beethoven
    C. Mozart

C Match the names with the descriptions. (6 points)

A		B
1. _____ Xavier Naidoo		A. traditional male singer
2. _____ Stefanie Hertl		B. group from Switzerland
3. _____ Reinhard Mey		C. male rock singer
4. _____ *Die Dissidenten*		D. singer of classical music
5. _____ Thomas Quasthoff		E. traditional female singer
6. _____ *Clepsydra*		F. group promoting world harmony

Unit 15

A Answer in complete sentences in German. (4 points)

1. Wie ist das Wetter im Winter?

   _____

2. Wie ist das Wetter im Sommer?

   _____

3. Wie ist das Wetter im Herbst?

   _____

4. Wie ist das Wetter im Frühling?

   _____

B Match the English weather expressions with the correct German expressions. (8 points)

A	B
1. _____ It's hot.	A Es regnet.
2. _____ It's cloudy.	B. die Jahreszeit
3. _____ It's raining.	C. Es ist kühl.
4. _____ It's windy.	D. Es ist windig.
5. _____ It's humid.	E. Es ist heiß.
6. _____ It's cool.	F. Es ist schwühl.
7. _____ the weather	G. das Wetter
8. _____ the season	H. Es ist wolkig.

 C Lies die Sätze und die Fragen. Wähle dann die richtigen Antworten. *(Read the sentences and the questions. Then circle the letters of the correct answers.)* (8 points)

1. Es donnert und blitzt. Paul ist zu Hause und ist traurig.
   Warum ist Paul traurig?
   A. Es ist schön.
   B. Es ist schlecht.

2. Es ist warm. Monika ist im Garten. Sie ist sehr glücklich.
   Warum ist Monika glücklich?
   A. Es ist schön.
   B. Es ist schlecht.

3. Es schneit und ich habe meine Handschuhe und meinen Hut an.
   Welche Jahreszeit haben wir?
   A. Sommer
   B. Winter

4. Es ist sehr warm.
   Welche Jahreszeit haben wir?
   A. Herbst
   B. Sommer

5. Ich trage meinen Regenschirm.
   Welche Jahreszeit haben wir?
   A. Frühling
   B. Winter

6. Es schneit viel und alles ist weiß.
   Welche Jahreszeit haben wir?
   A. Herbst
   B. Winter

7. Georg: Trage deine Sonnenbrille!
   Wie ist das Wetter?
   A. Es ist sonnig.
   B. Es regnet.

8. Die vier Jahreszeiten sind interessant.
   Wie viele Jahreszeiten gibt es?
   A. vier
   B. interessant

Unit 16

A **Beantworte jede Frage auf Deutsch!** *(Write a short answer to each question in German.)* **(4 points)**

1. Welcher Tag ist heute?

   _____

2. Was ist das Datum heute?

   _____

3. Wann hast du Geburtstag?

   _____

4. Was hast du morgen?

   _____

B **Schreib auf Deutsch!** *(Write these words in German.)* **(3 points)**

1. the month   _____
2. the day   _____
3. the week   _____

C **Verbinde die Wochentage mit der Mythologie.** *(Match the weekdays with the mythology.)* **(7 points)**

	A		B
1.	_____ Donnerstag	A.	Odin / Wodan
2.	_____ Sonntag	B.	Moon God
3.	_____ Dienstag	C.	seeds / harvest
4.	_____ Mittwoch	D.	Sun God
5.	_____ Samstag	E.	Freia
6.	_____ Freitag	F.	Tyr
7.	_____ Monday	G.	Thor

D Lies die Sätze und die Fragen! Dann wähle die richtigen Antworten (*Read the sentences and the questions. Then circle the letters of the correct answers.*) **(6 points)**

1. Wann ist die Party?
   A. Der Schultag.
   B. Übermorgen.

2. An welchem Tag ist der Feiertag?
   A. Am Dienstag.
   B. Die Woche.

3. Wann ist die Klavierstunde?
   A. Gestern.
   B. Am 13. August.

4. Was hast du am Donnerstag?
   A. Nichts. Ich habe frei.
   B. Der 30. September.

5. Was hast du heute?
   A. Eine Englischarbeit.
   B Montag.

6. Was ist das Datum morgen?
   A. Im Januar.
   B. Der fünfzehnte Mai.

Unit 17

A Identify the author of each work by choosing a name from the list. (6 points)

Else Lasker-Schüler
Christa Wolf
Sarah Kirsch
Johann Wolfgang von Goethe
Friedrich Schiller
Ernst Theodor Amadeus Hoffmann

1. *Wilhelm Tell*

   _____

2. *Landaufenthalt*

   _____

3. *Styx*

   _____

4. *Faust*

   _____

5. *Der geteilte Himmel*

   _____

6. *Nussknacker und Mausekönig*

   _____

B Match the descriptions with the literary works. (6 points)

A	B
1. _____ about a person's desire to know all the answers	A. *Styx; Der siebente Tag; Hebräische Balladen*
2. _____ about a girl's dream and a gift that becomes real	B. *Wilhelm Tell*
3. _____ about love, friendship and loss	C. *An die Freude*
4. _____ about a man's love of country and family	D. *Der geteilte Himmel*
5. _____ about a couple divided by politics	E. *Faust*
6. _____ about hope for a better world	F. *Nussknacker und Mausekönig*

C Identify each work below as poetry or play. (4 points)

1. *Wilhelm Tell*   _____

2. *Nussknacker und Mausekönig*   _____

3. *Hebräische Balladen*   _____

4. *Faust*   _____

D Who came from where? Name the author who came from each place listed. Choose from Schiller, Goethe, Wolf, and Lasker-Schüler. (4 points)

1. from Berlin   _____

2. from Marbach   _____

3. from Frankfurt   _____

4. from Landsberg   _____

Unit 18

A Complete the phrases and sentences by selecting words from the box. (5 points)

> Party   auch   ein
>
> Musik   klar

1. Ich _____!

2. Es gibt heute _____ Picknick.

3. Ich gehe auf die _____.

4. Gibt es da auch _____?

5. Na _____!

B Ergänze die Sätze. *(Write the German words in the spaces provided.)* (5 points)

1. Ich . . . gern . . . *(ride a bike)*   _____

2. Ich . . . gern. *(ride a horse)*   _____

3. Ich . . . gern. *(swim)*   _____

4. Ich . . . gern. *(read)*   _____

5. Ich . . . gern. *(dance)*   _____

C Read the questions. Then answer them by circling the letters of the correct answers. (6 points)

1. Wann gehst du ins Museum?
   A. Die Kunst.
   B. Morgen.
   C. Die *Alte Pinakothek.*

2. Wohin geht Ingrid heute?
   A. Zum Dürerfest.
   B. Na klar.
   C. Fußball.

3. Welche Sportart treibst du?
   A. Baseball ist ein Spiel.
   B. Ich spiele Baseball.
   C. Baseball ist schön.

4. Wo gibt es eine Party?
   A. Die Party ist um sieben Uhr.
   B. Ich gehe gern auf die Party.
   C. Die Party ist am Strand.

5. Wer geht zum Picknick?
   A. Josef.
   B. Um halb eins.
   C. Das Rad.

6. Willst du zum Spiel mitkommen?
   A. Ich laufe gern Ski.
   B. Elisabeth spielt Tennis mit Jürgen.
   C. Ja. Ich gehe gern zum Spiel.

D **Answer the questions in German. Write out complete sentences. (4 points)**

1. Wohin gehst du ?

   _____

2. Welche Sportart treibst du?

   _____

3. Was machst du gern in deiner Freizeit?

   _____

4. Gehst du heute zum Strand?

   _____

Unit 19

A Write the German words in the spaces provided. (5 points)

1. the salesclerk (m.)   _____

2. the customer (f.)   _____

3. the shopping center   _____

4. the shopping   _____

5. to buy   _____

B Circle the letter of English meaning that matches the German. (5 points)

1. Das Geld ist in der Kasse.
   A. The change is in my wallet.
   B. The money is in the cash register.

2. auf dem Markt
   A. at the market
   B. at the store

3. Ich kaufe ein.
   A. I pay.
   B. I shop.

4. Es ist billig.
   A. It's cheap.
   B. It's expensive.

5. Angebote
   A. special offers
   B. prices

C Choose the correct answers to each question. (6 points)

1. Wie viel kosten die Tennisschuhe?
   A. Im Geschäft.
   B. Vierzig Euro.

2. Was kaufst du dort?
   A. Zehn Pfirsiche.
   B. Zehn Euro.

3. Wie viele CDs hast du, Dieter?
   A. Drei.
   B. Teuer.

4. Ist das alles?
   A. Danke schön.
   B. Ja.

5. Wo sind die Tomaten?
   A. Die Tomaten sind auf dem Markt.
   B. Ich kaufe die Tomaten.

6. Was darf es sein?
   A. Es ist sehr teuer.
   B. Ich schaue mich nur um.

D **Write a complete answer in German to each question. (4 points)**

1. Wie viel kostet die DVD?

   _____

2. Wohin gehst du?

   _____

3. Ist das alles?

   _____

4. Wo ist das Geld?

   _____

Unit

A Write the German words. (5 points)

1. by ship   _____

2. by car   _____

3. the ticket   _____

4. the suitcase   _____

5. the street   _____

B Circle the letter of the English meaning that matches the German words. (6 points)

1. Rückfahrkarte
   A. roundtrip tichet
   B. second class ticket

2. Sie brauchen ihn, wenn Sie ankommen.
   A. But you must buy a ticket.
   B. You'll need it when you arrive.

3. Steigen Sie am Park aus!
   A. Wait at the park.
   B. Get off at the park.

4. Frau Müller ist am Schalter.
   A. Mrs. Müller is at the counter.
   B. Mrs. Müller is at the gate.

5. Der Angestellte spricht mit dem Reisenden.
   A. The employee is speaking with the traveler.
   B. The traveler is waiting at the train station.

6. Ich möchte kaufen . . .
   A. I'm going to travel . . .
   B. I would like to buy . . .

C Finish each sentence by choosing the letter of the correct completion. Write the letter to the left of each number. (6 points)

_____ 1. Herr Mendelssohn steigt in den . . . ein.   A. Fahrplan

_____ 2. Die . . . kauft eine Fahrkarte.   B. Straße

_____ 3. Hier ist der . . .   C. Reisende

_____ 4. Das Flugzeug ist auf dem . . .   D. Bahnhof

_____ 5. Der Zug ist in dem . . .   E. Flughafen

_____ 6. Es gibt viele Autos auf der . . .   F. Bus

D Write a complete answer for each question. (3 points)

1. Wie reist du?

_____

2. Wo ist Ihr Reisepass?

_____

3. Um wie viel Uhr fährt der Bus?

_____

Check-up Written Activities Answer Key

Unit 1

A. 1. Junge   2. Mädchen   3. Mädchen   4. Junge   5. Mädchen   6. Junge

B. 1. Englisch   2. Deutsch   3. bitte   4. Auf Wiedersehen!

C. 1. F   2. J   3. G   4. I   5. C   6. A   7. E   8. B   9. H   10. D

Unit 2

A. 1. das   2. eine   3. ein   4. eine   5. ein   6. Heft   7. Klasse   8. Kuli   9. Papier   10. Lineal

B. 1. A   2. B   3. C   4. C   5. B

C. 1. B   2. A   3. A   4. B   5. B

Unit 3

A. 1. 9   2. 21   3. 68   4. 33   5. 80

B. 1. B   2. B   3. A   4. C   5. C

C. *Answers will vary.*

D. 1. acht   2. zwanzig   3. zwei   4. sechzig   5. sechsunddreißig

Unit 4

A. 1. river   2. yes   3. southwest   4. mountain range   5. avalanches   6. east   7. the Baltic Sea   8. Austria   9. north   10. Switzerland and Austria

B. 1. D   2. A   3. B   4. E   5. C

C. 1. A   2. C   3. D   4. E   5. B

Unit 5

A. 1. das Haus   2. der Garten   3. das Wohnzimmer   4. die Terrasse   5. die Küche

B. 1. Mietshaus   2. Ich wohne   3. hinter   4. Wo   5. Schlafzimmer

C. 1. B   2. D   3. E   4. A   5. C

D. 1. wohnst   2. Zelt   3. Zimmer   4. Villa   5. Einfamilienhaus

Unit 6

A. 1. der Bruder   2. die Patin   3. die Kusine   4. der Enkel   5. die Frau   6. die Tochter

B. 1. A   2. B   3. B   4. A

C. 1. C   2. B   3. C   4. A   5. B   6. A   7. B   8. B   9. C   10. A

Unit 7

A. 1. Das ist eine Ziege.   2. Das ist ein Pferd.   3. Das ist ein Hund.   4. Das ist eine Katze.
5. Das ist ein Kaninchen.

B. 1. Lande   2. Teich   3. Stall   4. Weide   5. Luft

C. 1. A   2. A   3. B   4. A   5. B   6. A   7. A   8. B   9. B   10. A

Unit 8

A. 1. Koch   2. Musikerin   3. Briefträger   4. Geschäftsfrau   5. Krankenpflegerin
6. Programmierer   7. Tischler   8. Elektrikerin

B. 1. Ich bin Landwirt.   2. Ich bin Schauspielerin.   3. Ich bin Koch.
4. Ich bin Programmiererin.   5. Ich bin Lehrer.

C. 1. Ich bin Ärztin.   2. Ich bin Mechaniker.

D. 1. A   2. C   3. B

Unit 9

A. *Answers will vary.*

B. 1. A   2. B   3. B   4. A   5. B   6. A   7. C   8. B   9. A   10. C   11. C   12. A
13. B   14. A

Unit 10

A. *Answers will vary.*

B. 1. Expressionism   2. Classicism   3. Romanticism

C. 1. Friedrich   2. Votteler   3. Kirchner   4. Dietz   5. Dürer   6. Richter   7. Marc   8. Dürer

D. 1. C   2. B   3. D   4. A

Unit 11

A. 1. die Nase   2. das Ohr   3. das Auge   4. der Mund   5. das Bein   6. die Stirn   7. der Fuß
    8. der Ellenbogen

B. 1. I am sick.   2. Benjamin is sad.   3. You are happy.   4. I have a headache.

C. 1. Ich fühle mich gut (schlecht).   2. Es geht mir gut (schlecht). / Gut, danke. Und dir?
    3. Ja. Ich bin traurig. / Nein. Ich bin glücklich.   4. Ja. Rainer ist krank. / Nein. Rainer ist gesund.

Unit 12

A. 1. die Bluse   2. der Gürtel   3. der Bademantel   4. das Taschentuch   5. die Hose

B. *Sample Answers:*   1. Ich habe einen Anzug an. (Ich habe ein Kleid an.)   2. Ich habe eine Jacke
    an. (eine Strickjacke, einen Mantel)   3. Der Schlafanzug ist schön. (klein, groß)

C. 1. A   2. B   3. A   4. A   5. B

D. 1. D   2. B   3. A   4. C

Unit 13

A. 1. 1:00   2. 8:45   3. 7:10   4. 2:40   5. 10:30

B. 1. It is midnight.   2. It is noon.   3. At what time?

C. *Answers will vary.*

D. 1. A   2. B   3. B   4. A

E. 1. Farbe   2. Zeit   3. grau   4. rosa

Unit 14

A. 1. Bach   2. Beethoven   3. Mozart   4. Quasthoff

B. 1. A   2. B   3. A   4. C   5. B   6. C   7. B   8. A   9. C   10. B

C. 1. C   2. E   3. A   4. F   5. D   6. B

Unit 15

A. 1. Es ist kalt.   2. Es ist heiß.   3. Es ist kühl und windig.   4. Es ist kühl und es regnet.

B. 1. E   2. H   3. A   4. D   5. F   6. C   7. G   8. B

C. 1. B   2. A   3. B   4. B   5. A   6. B   7. A   8. A

Unit 16

A. *Answers will vary.*

B. 1. der Monat   2. der Tag   3. die Woche

C. 1. G   2. D   3. F   4. A   5. C   6. E   7. B

D. 1. B   2. A   3. B   4. A   5. A   6. B

Unit 17

A. 1. Friedrich Schiller   2. Sarah Kirsch   3. Else Lasker-Schüler
   4. Johann Wolfgang von Goethe   5. Christa Wolf   6. E.T.A. Hoffmann

B. 1. E   2. F   3. A   4. B   5. D   6. C

C. 1. play   2. story   3. poetry   4. play

D. 1. Lasker-Schüler   2. Schiller   3. Goethe   4. Wolf

Unit 18

A. 1. auch   2. ein   3. Party   4. Musik   5. klar

B. 1. fahre . . . Rad   2. reite   3. schwimme   4. lese   5. tanze

C. 1. B   2. A   3. B   4. C   5. A   6. C

D. *Answers will vary.*

Unit 19

A. 1. der Verkäufer   2. die Kundin   3. das Einkaufszentrum   4. das Einkaufen   5. kaufen

B. 1. B   2. A   3. B   4. A   5. A

C. 1. B   2. A   3. A   4. B   5. A   6. B

D. *Answers will vary.*

Unit 20

A. 1. mit dem Schiff   2. mit dem Auto   3. die Fahrkarte   4. der Koffer   5. die Straße

B. 1. A   2. B   3. B   4. A   5. A   6. B

C. 1. F   2. C   3. A   4. E   5. D   6. B

D. *Answers will vary.*

Check-up Listening Activities Program Manager

Content	Check-up Listening CD Number	Track	Time
Unit 1 Begrüßungen und Höflichkeit *(Greetings and Expressions of Courtesy)*			
Activity A	1	1	2:43
Activity B	1	2	1:02
Unit 2 Die Klasse und Imperative *(Classroom Objects and Commands)*			
Activity A	1	3	1:45
Activity B	1	4	1:50
Unit 3 Die Zahlen *(Numbers)*			
Activity A	1	5	1:28
Activity B	1	6	1:26
Activity C	1	7	1:18
Activity D	1	8	1:05
Unit 4 Die Geografie *(Geography)*			
Activity A	1	9	1:32
Activity B	1	10	1:15
Activity C	1	11	0:13
Unit 5 Das Haus *(House)*			
Activity A	1	12	1:06
Activity B	1	13	0:49
Activity C	1	14	1:02
Activity D	1	15	1:25
Unit 6 Die Familie *(Family)*			
Activity A	1	16	1:33
Activity B	1	17	1:30
Activity C	1	18	1:15
Unit 7 Die Tiere *(Animals)*			
Activity A	1	19	1:37
Activity B	1	20	1:27
Activity C	1	21	1:10
Activity D	1	22	0:46

Content	Check-up Listening CD Number	Track	Time
Unit 8 Die Berufe *(Occupations)*			
Activity A	1	23	1:41
Activity B	1	24	1:37
Activity C	1	25	0:44
Unit 9 Das Essen *(Food)*			
Activity A	1	26	1:40
Activity B	1	27	0:54
Activity C	1	28	1:31
Unit 10 Die Kunst *(Art)*			
Activity A	1	29	1:11
Activity B	1	30	1:05
Activity C	1	31	0:48
Activity D	1	32	1:12
Unit 11 Ker Körper und die Gesundheit *(Body and Health)*			
Activity A	2	1	3:39
Activity B	2	2	0:58
Activity C	2	3	0:43
Activity D	2	4	1:06
Unit 12 Die Kleidung *(Clothing)*			
Activity A	2	5	1:20
Activity B	2	6	1:38
Activity C	2	7	0:48
Activity D	2	8	0:45
Unit 13 Die Zeit und die Farben *(Time and Colors)*			
Activity A	2	9	1:34
Activity B	2	10	0:46
Activity C	2	11	1:04
Activity D	2	12	0:45
Unit 14 Die Musik *(Music)*			
Activity A	2	13	0:37
Activity B	2	14	1:28
Activity C	2	15	0:39
Activity D	2	16	1:13

Content	Check-up Listening CD Number	Track	Time
Unit 15 Das Wetter und die Jahreszeiten *(Weather and Seasons)*			
Activity A	2	17	0:56
Activity B	2	18	0:47
Activity C	2	19	1:05
Activity D	2	20	0:47
Unit 16 Die Tage und die Monate *(Days and Months)*			
Activity A	2	21	1:21
Activity B	2	22	1:28
Activity C	2	23	1:16
Activity D	2	24	0:43
Unit 17 Die Literatur *(Literature)*			
Activity A	2	25	1:14
Activity B	2	26	1:34
Activity C	2	27	0:58
Activity D	2	28	0:52
Unit 18 Die Freizeit *(Leisure and Recreation)*			
Activity A	2	29	0:57
Activity B	2	30	1:21
Activity C	2	31	1:01
Activity D	2	32	0:47
Unit 19 Das Einkaufen *(Shopping)*			
Activity A	2	33	1:32
Activity B	2	34	1:08
Activity C	2	35	1:04
Activity D	2	36	0:44
Unit 20 Das Reisen und der Verkehr *(Travel and Transportation)*			
Activity A	2	37	1:05
Activity B	2	38	1:15
Activity C	2	39	1:05
Activity D	2	40	1:01

Check-up Listening Activities

Unit

A **You will hear 15 statements, questions, or names in German. Identify what is being said by circling A or B. (15 points)**

1. You are wishing Anna . . .
   A. a nice evening.
   B. a nice day.

2. This means someone wants to . . .
   A. meet you.
   B. know how you're doing.

3. This means . . .
   A. I am sorry.
   B. I do not speak German.

4. This expression mean that I . . .
   A. am happy to meet you.
   B. wish you success.

5. This is said when you . . .
   A. wish to be excused for something you did.
   B. plan to see someone again tomorrow.

6. I say this when someone asks . . .
   A. about how I am.
   B. if I speak a certain language.

7. This means . . .
   A. Does she speak German?
   B. Do you speak German?

8. This is said . . .
   A. when you go away from someone.
   B. when you greet someone.

9. This word indicates that you . . .
   A. agree with something.
   B. disagree with something.

10. This word means "please" as well as . . .
    A. thank you.
    B. you are welcome.

11. This is a name for a . . .
    A. *Mädchen*
    B. *Junge*

12. This is a name for a . . .
    A. *Mädchen*
    B. *Junge*

13. This is a name for a . . .
    A. *Mädchen*
    B. *Junge*

14. This is a name for a . . .
    A. *Mädchen*
    B. *Junge*

15. This is a name for a . . .
    A. *Mädchen*
    B. *Junge*

B **You will hear some statements and questions. Choose the correct response for each by circling either A or B. (5 points)**

1. A. Auf Wiedersehen.
   B. Ich heiße Elisabeth.

2. A. Nein. Ich spreche nicht russisch.
   B. Entchuldigung. Es tut mir leid.

3. A. Gute Nacht, Klaus!
   B. Guten Morgen, Herr Meyer!

4. A. Bis morgen!
   B. Tag!

5. A. Nein.
   B. Gut, danke.

Unit 2

A You will hear ten statements in German that describe something related to school. Circle the letter of the correct picture. (10 points)

1. A.   B.

2. A.   B.

3. A.    B.

4. A.    B.

5. A.    B.

6. A.   B.

7. A.   B.

8. A.

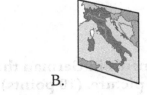 B.

9. A.

B.

10. A.

B.

B You will hear ten classroom commands. Identify each one by circling either A or B. (10 points)

1. A. Open your book.
   B. Answer the question.

2. A. Draw a picture.
   B. Listen.

3. A. Speak.
   B. Complete.

4. A. Listen.
   B. Read.

5. A. Write.
   B. Repeat.

6. A. Close the book.
   B. Open the book.

7. A. Complete the sentences.
   B. Raise your hand.

8. A. Say it in German.
   B. Complete the sentences.

9. A. Turn the computer off.
   B. Turn the computer on.

10. A. Take paper out.
    B. Go to the board.

Unit 3

A You will hear ten numbers in German. Write down each one with an Arabic numeral. (5 points)

> **Beispiel:** You hear: neunzehn
> You write: <u>19</u>

1. _____
2. _____
3. _____
4. _____
5. _____
6. _____
7. _____
8. _____
9. _____
10. _____

B You will hear six words or expressions. Identify what you hear by circling the letter of the correct answer. (3 points)

1. A. minus
   B. and or plus
   C. how much are
   D. divided by

2. A. and or plus
   B. how much are
   C. multiplied by
   D. numbers

3. A. how many
   B. divided by
   C. less or minus
   D. how

4. A. How much does something cost?
   B. How many books are there?
   C. How much is one and one?
   D. How many pens do you have?

5. A. and or plus
   B. multiplied by 30
   C. divided by
   D. minus or less

6. A. How much is a notebook?
   B. How much does the notebook cost?
   C. How many notebooks are there?
   D. How many notebooks do you have?

C Next you will hear the number of eight items. As you listen to the words, write down the corresponding Arabic numerals in the spaces provided. (8 points)

1. _____ Schreibtische

2. _____ Filzstifte

3. _____ Kulis

4. _____ Bücher

5. _____ Fenster

6. _____ Hefte

7. _____ Landkarten

8. _____ Lineale

D Identify the type of math problem you hear. Place a check mark in the column of the correct operation. (4 points)

+	−	×	÷
1. _____	_____	_____	_____
2. _____	_____	_____	_____
3. _____	_____	_____	_____
4. _____	_____	_____	_____

Name _____   Datum _____

Unit

A You will hear the name of a city. Decide in which country it is located. Place a check mark in the column of the correct country. (10 points)

	Österreich	die Schweiz	Deutschland
1.	_____	_____	_____
2.	_____	_____	_____
3.	_____	_____	_____
4.	_____	_____	_____
5.	_____	_____	_____
6.	_____	_____	_____
7.	_____	_____	_____
8.	_____	_____	_____
9.	_____	_____	_____
10.	_____	_____	_____

B Determine what the following words identify: a city, a river, or a mountain range. Place a check mark in the correct column. (8 points)

	City	River	Mountain Range
1.	_____	_____	_____
2.	_____	_____	_____
3.	_____	_____	_____
4.	_____	_____	_____
5.	_____	_____	_____
6.	_____	_____	_____
7.	_____	_____	_____
8.	_____	_____	_____

C Write the English equivalents of the words you hear. (2 points)

1. _____

2. _____

Unit

A **You will hear four questions. Circle the letter of the correct answer. (4 points)**

1. A. Das Haus ist da drüben.
   B. Ich esse in dem Garten.
   C. Ich wohne in Berlin.
   D. Es gibt sieben Zimmer.

2. A. Das ist die Villa.
   B. Ich wohne in Köln.
   C. Er is da drüben.
   D. Ich spiele in dem Spielzimmer.

3. A. Sie ist hinter dem Garten.
   B. Es gibt fünf Zimmer.
   C. Ich wohne in Innsbruck.
   D. Das ist die Garage.

4. A. Die Küche ist da drüben.
   B. Das ist das Mietshaus.
   C. Das Esszimmer ist hinter dem Wohnzimmer.
   D. Es gibt neun Zimmer.

B **You will hear five place names in German. Circle the letter of the correct picture. (5 points)**

1. A. 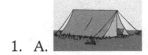   B.

2. A.    B.

3. A.    B.

4. A.    B.

5. A.  B.

C You will hear the descriptions of five places in English. Which German place does each identify? Circle the letter of the correct answer. (5 points)

1. A. die Villa
   B. die Zimmer im Haus
   C. die Hütte

2. A. die Garage
   B. das Badezimmer
   C. das Schlafzimmer

3. A. das Badezimmer
   B. das Mietshaus
   C. der Garten

4. A. das Haus
   B. die Wohnung
   C. das Zelt

5. A. die Villa
   B. das Einfamilienhaus
   C. die Hütte

D Complete the statements that you hear. Write the name of the room that best finishes each statement. (6 points)

1. _____

2. _____

3. _____

4. _____

5. _____

6. _____

Unit 6

A *Wer ist das?* **Identify the persons you hear. Choose the letter of the correct answer. (8 points)**

1. A. brother
   B. grandson
   C. female cousin

2. A. godmother
   B. sister
   C. child

3. A. aunt
   B. nephew
   C. mother

4. A. grandmother
   B. father
   C. female cousin

5. A. godmother
   B. male cousin
   C. grandson

6. A. girl
   B. aunt
   C. sister

7. A. son
   B. father
   C. godfather

8. A. nephew
   B. granddaughter
   C. uncle

B **What is the relationship? Which description best tells who this person is? Choose the letter of the correct answer. (5 points)**

1. A. daughter of my aunt
   B. sister of my mother
   C. daughter of my grandmother

2. A. the father of my father
   B. the brother of my father
   C. the nephew of my father

3. A. the brother of my mother
   B. the godfather of my mother
   C. the son of my mother

4. A. the daughter of my sister
   B. the mother of my cousin
   C. the aunt of my mother

5. A. the sister of my godmother
   B. the brother of my father
   C. the daughter of my daughter

C **Write the definite article *der*, *die*, or *das* for each noun you hear. (7 points)**

1. _____

2. _____

3. _____

4. _____

5. _____

6. _____

7. _____

Unit 7

A **Which animal is it? You will hear the German name of an animal. Circle the letter of the correct picture. (10 points)**

1. A.  B.  C.

2. A.  B.   C.

3. A.  B.  C.

4. A.  B.  C.

5. A.  B.  C.

6. A.  B.  C.

7. A.  B. 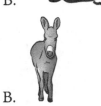 C.

8. A.  B.  C.

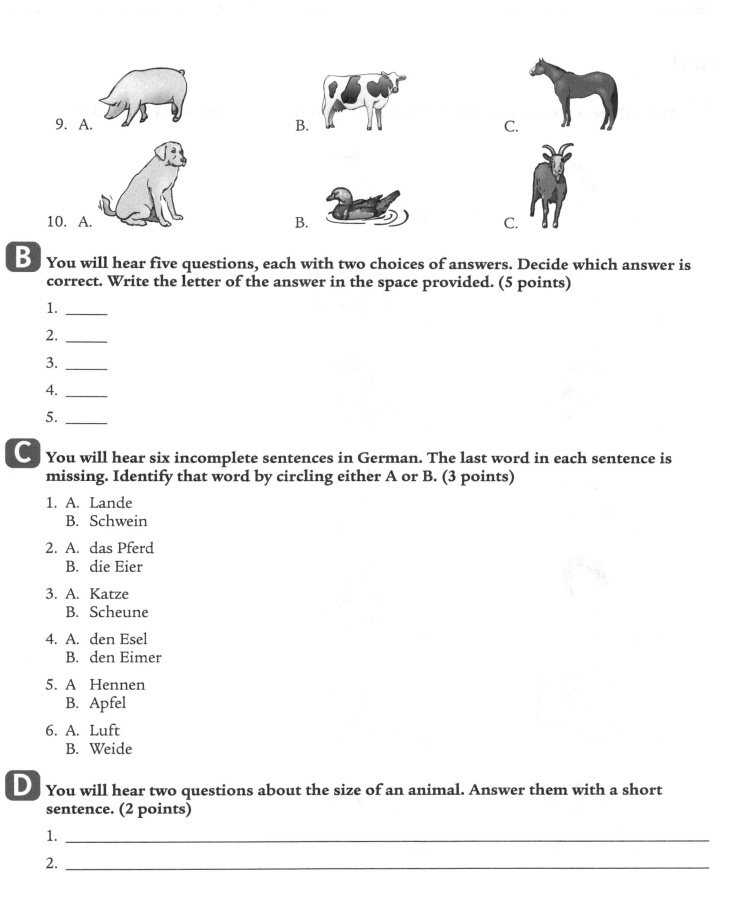

9. A.   B.   C.

10. A.   B.   C.

B You will hear five questions, each with two choices of answers. Decide which answer is correct. Write the letter of the answer in the space provided. (5 points)

1. _____

2. _____

3. _____

4. _____

5. _____

C You will hear six incomplete sentences in German. The last word in each sentence is missing. Identify that word by circling either A or B. (3 points)

1. A. Lande
   B. Schwein

2. A. das Pferd
   B. die Eier

3. A. Katze
   B. Scheune

4. A. den Esel
   B. den Eimer

5. A Hennen
   B. Apfel

6. A. Luft
   B. Weide

D You will hear two questions about the size of an animal. Answer them with a short sentence. (2 points)

1. _____

2. _____

Unit **8**

A You will hear ten occupations. Circle the letter of the correct picture. (10 points)

1. A.    B.

2. A.    B.

3. A.   B.

4. A.    B.

5. A.    B.

6. A.    B.

7. A.    B.

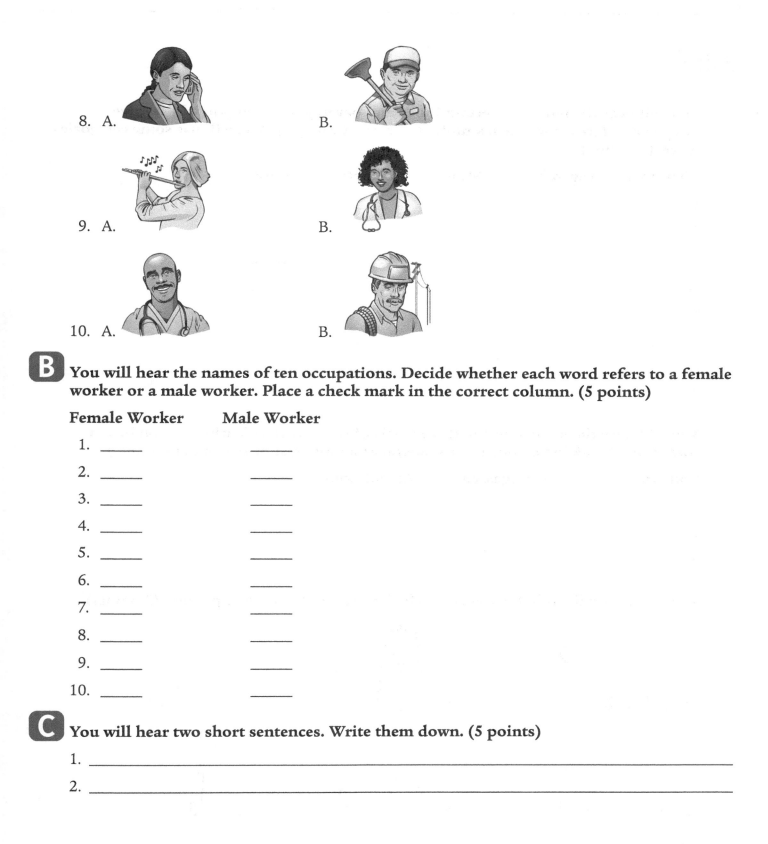

8. A.   B.

9. A.   B.

10. A.   B.

B You will hear the names of ten occupations. Decide whether each word refers to a female worker or a male worker. Place a check mark in the correct column. (5 points)

Female Worker   **Male Worker**

1. _____   _____
2. _____   _____
3. _____   _____
4. _____   _____
5. _____   _____
6. _____   _____
7. _____   _____
8. _____   _____
9. _____   _____
10. _____   _____

C You will hear two short sentences. Write them down. (5 points)

1. _____

2. _____

Unit 9

A You will hear the names of certain foods and beverages. Below you will see five categories. Place a check mark under the correct category. You will use some categories twice. (8 points)

	Beverage	Vegetable	Meat	Dessert	Fruit
1.	_____	_____	_____	_____	_____
2.	_____	_____	_____	_____	_____
3.	_____	_____	_____	_____	_____
4.	_____	_____	_____	_____	_____
5.	_____	_____	_____	_____	_____
6.	_____	_____	_____	_____	_____
7.	_____	_____	_____	_____	_____
8.	_____	_____	_____	_____	_____

B You will hear the menus for the three meals of the day. Decide whether you hear a traditional breakfast menu, a lunch menu, or a dinner/supper menu. (3 points)

Frühstück	Mittagessen	Abendessen
1. _____	_____	_____
2. _____	_____	_____
3. _____	_____	_____

C You will hear a list of table items. Circle the letter of the correct picture. (9 points)

1. A.   B.    C.

2. A.    B.   C.

3. A.  B.   C.

4. A.  B.  C.

5. A.  B.  C.

6. A.  B.  C.

7. A.  B.  C.

8. A. 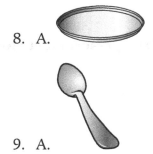 B.  C.

9. A.   B.   C.

Unit 10

A You will hear a description of a painting. Place a check mark in the column of the artist who created it. (6 points)

Dietz	Dürer	Friedrich	Kirchner	Marc	Votteler
1. _____	_____	_____	_____	_____	_____
2. _____	_____	_____	_____	_____	_____
3. _____	_____	_____	_____	_____	_____
4. _____	_____	_____	_____	_____	_____
5. _____	_____	_____	_____	_____	_____
6. _____	_____	_____	_____	_____	_____

B You will hear the names of four famous artists. Select the description of the style used by that person. Select your answers using the letters A, B, C, or D. (4 points)

Select from:

A. details and realistic proportions

B. bold heavy dark outlines, animals

C. landscapes and seascapes

D. cartoon-like people, social criticism

1. _____

2. _____

3. _____

4. _____

C You will hear four different kinds of artwork. Select the letter of the person most closely associated with each one. (4 points)

Select from:

A. Franz Marc

B. Caspar David Friedrich

C. Albrecht Dürer

D. Jutta Votteler

1. _____

2. _____

3. _____

4. _____

D **Write down the words you hear. (6 points)**

1. _____
2. _____
3. _____
4. _____
5. _____
6. _____

Unit 11

A Listen and identify each part of the body you hear by writing the corresponding letter on the line. (8 points)

1. _____
2. _____
3. _____
4. _____
5. _____
6. _____
7. _____
8. _____
9. _____
10. _____
11. _____
12. _____
13. _____
14. _____
15. _____
16. _____

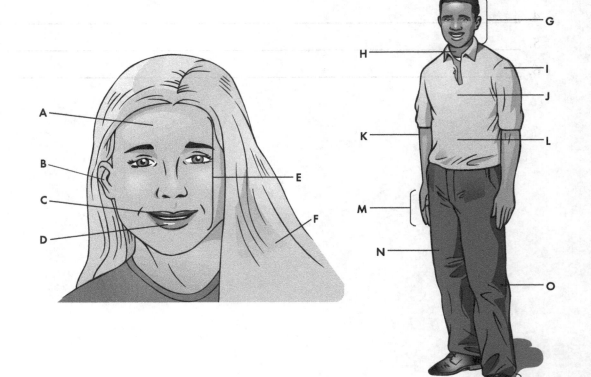

B You will hear the words for four parts of the body. Each item consists of a definite article and a noun. Write each German article and noun. (4 points)

1. _____   _____
2. _____   _____
3. _____   _____
4. _____   _____

C You will hear three words. Write the opposite of each word. (3 points)

1. _____
2. _____
3. _____

D **You will hear five questions. Circle the letter of the correct response. (5 points)**

1. A. Es geht mir gut.
   B. Hans ist krank.

2. A. Du bist krank.
   B. Ich habe Kopfweh.

3. A. Nein. Sie ist heute nicht krank.
   B. Nein. Ich bin heute gesund.

4. A. Gabriele ist traurig.
   B. Ich fühle mich wohl.

5. A. Ich habe Kopfweh.
   B. Nein. Ich bin glücklich.

Unit 12

A Listen and circle the letter of the correct clothing picture. (8 points)

1. A.   B.   C.

2. A.   B.   C.

3. A.   B.   C.

4. A.   B.   C.

5. A.   B.   C.

6. A.   B.   C.

7. A.   B.   C.

8. A.   B.   C.

B You will hear six sentences. On your answer sheet you will have a question relating to each one and three choices of answers. Answer each question by circling the letter of the correct answer. (6 points)

1. What do I want to do?
   A. play ball with a friend
   B. talk on the phone with a friend
   C. go someplace with a friend

2. What will I be doing soon?
   A. traveling
   B. shopping
   C. painting

3. What does someone tell me?
   A. not to wear something
   B. not to forget something
   C. not to go somewhere

4. Where am I going?
   A. to a musical event
   B. to a carnival
   C. to a tennis match

5. What must I do?
   A. buy a jacket
   B. go get my jacket
   C. borrow a jacket

6. What am I doing?
   A. ironing my clothes
   B. hanging up my suit
   C. packing my suitcase

C You will hear four articles of clothing or accessories. Pick the situation or time when each is appropriate. (4 points)

1. A. in the school cafeteria
   B. at bedtime
   C. during sports practice

2. A. in cold weather
   B. in hot weather
   C. in the movie theater

3. A. while swimming
   B. while sleeping
   C. while shoveling

4. A. to cover your head
   B. to lace up athletic shoes
   C. to secure a pair of pants

D You will hear two questions. Write a short answer in German to each. (2 points)

1. _____

2. _____

Unit 13

A You will hear eight times of day. Write down the numerical equivalent of what you hear. (8 points)

1. _____   5. _____

2. _____   6. _____

3. _____   7. _____

4. _____   8. _____

B You will hear four colors. Identify each one by circling the letter of the correct translation. (4 points)

1. A. blue
   B. white
   C. black

2. A. pink
   B. orange
   C. blue

3. A. gray
   B. brown
   C. red

4. A. yellow
   B. black
   C. green

C You will hear four questions. Answer each by circling the letter of the correct response. (4 points)

1. A. Der Elefant ist rosa.
   B. Der Elefant ist grau.
   C. Der Elefant ist blau.

2. A. Die Tiger sind schwarz und orange.
   B. Die Tiger sind rosa und grau.
   C. Die Tiger sind braun und violett.

3. A. Das Picknick ist fantastisch.
   B. Das Picknick ist für die Kinder.
   C. Das Picknick ist um halb zwei.

4. A. Es ist grün.
   B. Zeit und Farben.
   C. Ja. Es ist 12 Uhr.

D You will hear two questions. Write out a complete answer to both. (4 points)

1. _____

2. _____

Name _____   Datum _____

Unit 14

A You will hear the first names of three composers. Put a check mark in the column with the last name of each composer. (3 points)

Bach	Beethoven	Mozart
1. _____	_____	_____
2. _____	_____	_____
3. _____	_____	_____

B You will hear seven words or names. Identify each one by circling the letter of the correct description. (7 points)

1. A. birthplace of Beethoven   B. birthplace of Bach   C. birthplace of Mozart
2. A. ballet   B. opera   C. chamber music
3. A. concerto   B. opera   C. choral music
4. A. chamber music   B. choral music   C. symphony
5. A. songs   B. instrumental music   C. dances
6. A. birthplace of Mozart   B. birthplace of Beethoven   C. birthplace of Bach
7. A. The Magic Flute   B. The 6th Symphony   C. The Mass in B Minor

C You will hear the names of three works. Place a check mark in the column for the appropriate style of each work. (3 points)

Baroque	Romantic	Classical
1. _____	_____	_____
2. _____	_____	_____
3. _____	_____	_____

D You will hear names from the world of contemporary music. Determine whether each name refers to A (a singer) or B (a musical group). (7 points)

Select from:

A. singer

B. musical group

1. _____   5. _____
2. _____   6. _____
3. _____   7. _____
4. _____

Unit 15

A You will hear five weather reports. On your paper you have two categories of weather. Place a check mark in the correct column. **(5 points)**

	A. Es ist schön.	B. Es ist schlecht.
1.	_____	_____
2.	_____	_____
3.	_____	_____
4.	_____	_____
5.	_____	_____

B You will hear four words or expressions. Write the English meaning of each. **(4 points)**

1. _____

2. _____

3. _____

4. _____

C You will hear five sentences. Choose the logical association or response for each. **(5 points)**

1. A. Trage deinen Regenschirm!
   B. Trage deine Sonnenbrille!

2. A. Trage deinen Hut und deinen Mantel!
   B. Trage deinen Regenschirm!

3. A. Trage deine Sonnenbrille!
   B. Trage deinen Regenschirm!

4. A. Es ist schwühl.
   B. Es schneit.

5. A. Es ist warm.
   B. Es ist kalt.

D You will hear two questions. Answer each one in a complete sentence in German. **(6 points)**

1. _____

2. _____

Unit 16

A You will hear dates. Write down each one in number form. Remember that the day always goes before the month. (3 points)

1. _____

2. _____

3. _____

4. _____

5. _____

6. _____

B You will hear eight German words. Identify each one by circling the letter of the correct answer. (8 points)

1. A. school day
   B. holiday
   C. weekend

2. A. today
   B. tomorrow
   C. yesterday

3. A. month
   B. day
   C. weekend

4. A. day named after the god of war
   B. day named after the god of the moon
   C. day named after the goddess of love

5. A. day after tomorrow
   B. yesterday
   C. today

6. A. birthday
   B. day after tomorrow
   C. today

7. A. day named after the god of the sun
   B. day named after the god of harvest
   C. day named after the god of weather

8. A. first month
   B. sixth month
   C. twelfth month

C You will hear seven questions. Circle the letter of the correct answer. (7 points)

1. A. Der 5. September.
   B. Ich habe gar nichts.

2. A. 18.5.
   B. Morgen.

3. A. Ja.
   B. Der Montag.

4. A. Ich habe heute frei.
   B. Übermorgen.

5. A. Ein Tag.
   B. Ein Monat.

6. A. Am 3. Oktober.
   B. Das Datum.

7. A. Ein Monat.
   B. Ein Tag.

D Write a short answer in German to each question. (2 points)

1. _____

2. _____

Unit 17

A Match the sounds you hear with the words you see. You will hear the German titles of literary works, labeled A through F. Match each title you hear with the words. Write the appropriate letter in the space provided. (6 points)

1. *Styx* _____
2. *Der geteilte Himmel* _____
3. *Maria Stuart* _____
4. *Landaufenthalt* _____
5. *Nussknacker und Mausekönig* _____
6. *Faust* _____

B You will hear six clues as to the identity of six great authors. They will be labeled A through F. Write the letter of each clue next to the name it matches. (6 points)

1. Else Lasker-Schüler _____
2. Christa Wolf _____
3. Friedrich Schiller _____
4. Johann Wolfgang von Goethe _____
5. Sarah Kirsch _____
6. Ernst Theodor Amadeus Hoffmann _____

C You will hear the names of four works. What kind of literary work is each? Place a check mark in the correct column. (4 points)

	Novel	Poetry	Play	Story
1.	_____	_____	_____	_____
2.	_____	_____	_____	_____
3.	_____	_____	_____	_____
4.	_____	_____	_____	_____

D You will hear the names of four places. Which place is associated with each author? Place a check mark in the column of the correct author. (4 points)

	Hoffmann	Schiller	Elsa Lasker-Schüler	Goethe
1.	_____	_____	_____	_____
2.	_____	_____	_____	_____
3.	_____	_____	_____	_____
4.	_____	_____	_____	_____

Name _____   Datum _____

Unit 18

A You will hear five nouns in German. Circle the letter of the correct association. (5 points)

1. A. das Dürerfest
   B. das Museum
   C. das Spiel

2. A. Alte Pinakothek
   B. das Rad
   C. das Picknick

3. A. Ich tanze.
   B. Ich schwimme.
   C. Ich laufe Ski.

4. A. lesen
   B. reiten
   C. tanzen

5. A. Ich lese.
   B. Ich reite.
   C. Ich spiele.

B You will hear six questions. Each one has three choices of replies. Circle the letter of the correct response. (6 points)

1. A. Zum Volleyballspiel.
   B. Heute Abend.
   C. Nein.

2. A. Ich gehe ins Museum.
   B. Ich reite gern.
   C. Na klar.

3. A. Die Freizeit.
   B. Das Dürerfest.
   C. Die Sportart.

4. A. Zum Strand.
   B. Heute Abend.
   C. Ja.

5. A. Es gibt ein Dürerfest im Museum.
   B. Nein. Ich gehe zum Spiel.
   C. Ich höre gern Musik.

6. A. Nein.
   B. Ins Museum.
   C. Die Freizeit.

C You will hear the beginning of five sentences. Circle the letter of the best completion. (5 points)

1. A. Ich auch.
   B. ins Museum
   C. Basketballspiel

2. A. statt
   B. los
   C. wo

3. A. Baseball
   B. Volleyball
   C. Rad

4. A. nein
   B. gern
   C. mitkommen

5. A. das Picknick
   B. die Party
   C. mein Buch

D You will hear two questions. Answer each one in a complete sentence. *Auf Deutsch, bitte!* (4 points)

1. _____

2. _____

Unit 19

A You will hear eight words. Circle the letter of the correct English equivalent. (8 points)

1. A. saleswoman
   B. male customer
   C. salesman

2. A. cashier
   B. cash register
   C. change

3. A. price
   B. money
   C. change

4. A. shopping center
   B. selection
   C. customer

5. A. reduced price
   B. expensive
   C. cheap

6. A. peaches
   B. selection
   C. customer

7. A. to cost
   B. to buy
   C. to shop

8. A. change
   B. shopping center
   C. store

B You will hear five words in German. Write each one down. Be sure to include the definite article. (5 points)

1. _____

2. _____

3. _____

4. _____

5. _____

C You will hear five questions or statements. Circle the letter of the best reply. (5 points)

1. A. Drei Tomaten.
   B. Danke schön.
   C. Zum Einkaufszentrum.

2. A. Tennisschuhe.
   B. Grüne Bohnen.
   C. Verkäufer.

3. A. Ich möchte eine CD kaufen.
   B. Hier ist das Geld.
   C. Sie kostet zehn Euro.

4. A. Ich kaufe auf dem Markt ein.
   B. Sie sind auf dem Markt.
   C. Nein. Sie sind nicht billig.

5. A. Das ist billig.
   B. Ja. Ich möchte Tennisschuhe.
   C. Unsere Auswahl ist sehr groß.

D You will hear two questions. Answer each in a complete sentence in German. (2 points)

1. _____

2. _____

Unit

A You will hear six phrases. Circle the letter of the correct English equivalent. (6 points)

1. A. by train
   B. by car
   C. by bus

2. A. I travel.
   B. I fly.
   C. I get off.

3. A. at the airport
   B. at the bus station
   C. at the train station

4. A. at the airlines counter
   B. at the bus stop
   C. at passport control

5. A. a one-way ticket
   B. a round-trip ticket
   C. a discounted ticket

6. A. at 2 o'clock
   B. second class
   C. on the left

B You will hear six words with their definite articles. Write down each word including *der, die,* or *das.* (6 points)

1. _____

2. _____

3. _____

4. _____

5. _____

6. _____

You will hear five questions. Circle the letter of the best reply. (5 points)

1. A. Auf der Straße.
   B. Auf dem Bahnhof.
   C. Auf dem Flughafen.

2. A. Um 14 Uhr.
   B. Am Park.
   C. Mit dem Auto.

3. A. Sie brauchen ihn, wenn Sie ankommen.
   B. Fahren Sie mit dem Bus Nummer zwei!
   C. Das macht € 200.

4. A. Hier ist die Fahrkarte.
   B. Die Fahrkarte kostet € 70.
   C. Ich kaufe eine Fahrkarte.

5. A. Ja, das ist ein Schiff.
   B. Das Schiff ist groß.
   C. Das Schiff ist da drüben.

D **You will hear three questions. Answer each in a complete sentence in German. (3 points)**

1. _____

2. _____

3. _____

Check-up Listening Activities Answer Key

Unit 1

A You will hear 15 statements, questions, or names in German. Identify what is being said by circling A or B. (15 points)

1.	Guten Abend, Anna!	A
2.	Wie geht's?	B
3.	Es tut mir leid.	A
4.	Angenehm. Es freut mich.	A
5.	Bis morgen!	B
6.	Nicht schlecht.	A
7.	Sprichst du deutsch?	B
8.	Auf Wiedersehen!	A
9.	Ja.	A
10.	Bitte.	B
11.	Dieter	B
12.	Susanne	A
13.	Niklas	B
14.	Karsten	B
15.	Petra	A

B You will hear some statements and questions. Choose the correct response for each by circling either A or B. (5 points)

1.	Ich heiße Florian.	B
2.	Du sprichst russisch, nicht wahr?	A
3.	Guten Morgen, Herr Fischer!	B
4.	Gute Nacht!	A
5.	Wie geht's?	B

A You will hear ten statements in German that describe something related to school. Circle the letter of the correct picture. (10 points)

1. Das ist eine Uhr. **A**

2. Das ist ein Kuli. **B**

3. Das ist eine Landkarte. **A**

4. Das ist ein Filzstift. **A**

5. Das ist ein Heft. **B**

6. Das ist ein Blatt Papier. **A**

7. Das ist eine Tafel. **B**

8. Das ist ein Wischer. **A**

9. Das ist ein Fenster. **A**

10. Das ist eine Tastatur. **A**

B You will hear ten classroom commands. Identify each one by circling either A or B. (10 points)

1. Beantworte die Frage! **B**

2. Hör zu! **B**

3. Sprich! **A**

4. Lies! **B**

5. Schreib! **A**

6. Mach das Buch zu! **A**

7. Heb die Hand! **B**

8. Ergänze die Sätze! **B**

9. Schalte den Computer aus! **A**

10. Geh an die Tafel! **B**

Unit 3

A You will hear ten numbers in German. Write down each one with an Arabic numeral. (5 points)

1.	drei	**3**
2.	sechs	**6**
3.	elf	**11**
4.	zwölf	**12**
5.	siebzehn	**17**
6.	achtundzwanzig	**28**
7.	einunddreißig	**31**
8.	sechsundvierzig	**46**
9.	fünfundfünzig	**55**
10.	zweiundsechzig	**62**

B You will hear six words or expressions. Identify what you hear by circling the letter of the correct answer. (3 points)

1.	geteilt durch	**D**
2.	und	**A**
3.	weniger	**C**
4.	Wie viele Bücher gibt es?	**B**
5.	mal dreißig	**B**
6.	Wie viel ist ein Heft?	**A**

C Next you will hear the number of eight items. As you listen to the words, write down the corresponding Arabic numerals in the spaces provided. (8 points)

1. fünfundzwanzig Schreibtische   **25**
2. zehn Filzstifte   **10**
3. vierzehn Kulis   **14**
4. achtundsiebzig Bücher   **78**
5. vier Fenster   **4**
6. siebenunddreißig Hefte   **37**
7. zwei Landkarten   **2**
8. sechsundzwanzig Lineale   **26**

D Identify the type of math problem you hear. Place a check mark in the column of the correct operation. (4 points)

1. Sieben mal drei ist einundzwanzig.   ×
2. Fünfundvierzig geteilt durch neun ist fünf.   ÷
3. Elf weniger zwei ist neun.   −
4. Drei und zwölf ist fünfzehn.   +

Unit 4

A

You will hear the name of a city. Decide in which country it is located. Place a check mark in the column of the correct country. (10 points)

1.	Berlin	**Deutschland**
2.	Bern	**die Schweiz**
3.	Köln	**Deutschland**
4.	Zürich	**die Schweiz**
5.	Salzburg	**Österreich**
6.	Leipzig	**Deutschland**
7.	Genf	**die Schweiz**
8.	München	**Deutschland**
9.	Wien	**Österreich**
10.	Frankfurt	**Deutschland**

B

Determine what the following words identify: a city, a river, or a mountain range. Place a check mark in the correct column. (8 points)

1.	die Donau	**River**
2.	der Harz	**Mountain Range**
3.	Frankfurt	**City**
4.	die Alpen	**Mountain Range**
5.	Salzburg	**City**
6.	die Elbe	**River**
7.	Berlin	**City**
8.	der Rhein	**River**

C

Write the English equivalents of the words you hear. (2 points)

1.	die Ostsee	**the Baltic Sea**
2.	die Donau	**the Danube (River)**

Unit 5

A
You will hear four questions. Circle the letter of the correct answer. (4 points)

1. Wo wohnst du?   **C**

2. Wo ist der Garten?   **C**

3. Wo ist die Garage?   **A**

4. Wie viele Zimmer gibt es in deinem Haus?   **D**

B
You will hear five place names in German. Circle the letter of the correct picture. (5 points)

1. das Zelt   **A**

2. die Hütte   **B**

3. das Haus   **B**

4. die Wohnung   **A**

5. das Mietshaus   **B**

C
You will hear the descriptions of five places in English. Which German place does each identify? Circle the letter of the correct answer. (5 points)

1. fancy house   **A**

2. room in which to sleep   **C**

3. room in which to brush your teeth   **A**

4. rental unit in which to live   **B**

5. simple country lodge   **C**

D
Complete the statements that you hear. Write the name of the room that best finishes each statement. (6 points)

1. Ich koche in der . . .   **Küche**

2. Ich esse in dem . . .   **Esszimmer**

3. Ich wohne in dem . . .   **Wohnzimmer**

4. Ich bade in dem . . .   **Badezimmer**

5. Ich schlafe in dem . . .   **Schlafzimmer**

6. Das Auto ist in der . . .   **Garage**

Unit 6

A
Wer ist das? **Identify the persons you hear. Choose the letter of the correct answer. (8 points)**

1. der Bruder   **A**
2. die Patin   **A**
3. der Neffe   **B**
4. die Kusine   **C**
5. der Enkel   **C**
6. die Tante   **B**
7. der Sohn   **A**
8. der Onkel   **C**

B
What is the relationship? Which description best tells who this person is? Choose the letter of the correct answer. (5 points)

1. meine Tante   **B**
2. mein Cousin   **C**
3. mein Onkel   **A**
4. meine Nichte   **A**
5. meine Enkelin   **C**

C
Write the definite article *der*, *die*, or *das* for each noun you hear. (7 points)

1. Mutter   **die**
2. Tochter   **die**
3. Vater   **der**
4. Mädchen   **das**
5. Pate   **der**
6. Baby   **das**
7. Familie   **die**

Unit 7

A
Which animal is it? You will hear the German name of an animal. Circle the letter of the correct picture. (10 points)

1. das Kaninchen — **B**
2. die Henne — **A**
3. die Kuh — **B**
4. der Esel — **B**
5. die Katze — **C**
6. das Pferd — **A**
7. die Ente — **C**
8. der Vogel — **B**
9. das Schwein — **A**
10. die Ziege — **C**

B
You will hear five questions, each with two choices of answers. Decide which answer is correct. Write the letter of the answer in the space provided. (5 points)

1. Wo ist der Esel? — **B**
   A. In der Luft.
   B. Im Stall.

2. Wo ist die Kuh? — **B**
   A. Auf dem Teich.
   B. Auf der Weide.

3. Wo sind die Hennen? — **A**
   A. Hinter der Scheune.
   B. In der Luft.

4. Wo sind die Schweine? — **B**
   A. In dem Eimer.
   B. Im Stall.

5. Wo sind die Enten? — **A**
   A. Auf dem Teich.
   B. Auf der Weide.

C You will hear six incomplete sentences in German. The last word in each sentence is missing. Identify that word by circling either A or B. (3 points)

1. Jutta und Simon sind auf dem . . .   **A**

2. Simon sammelt die . . .   **B**

3. Wie heißt die . . . ?   **A**

4. Ich füttre . . .   **A**

5. Gibt es auch . . . ?   **A**

6. Die Kühe sind auf der . . .   **B**

D You will hear two questions about the size of an animal. Answer them with a short sentence. (2 points)

1. Wie ist Max, das Pferd?   **Max ist groß.**

2. Ist die Katze klein?   **Ja. Die Katze ist klein.**

Unit 8

A You will hear ten occupations. Circle the letter of the correct picture. (10 points)

1. der Mechaniker **A**
2. die Künstlerin **B**
3. die Briefträgerin **A**
4. der Krankenpfleger **B**
5. die Ärztin **A**
6. die Lehrerin **B**
7. der Landwirt **A**
8. der Geschäftsmann **A**
9. die Musikerin **A**
10. der Elektriker **B**

B You will hear the names of ten occupations. Decide whether each word refers to a female worker or a male worker. Place a check mark in the correct column. (5 points)

1. Mechaniker **male**
2. Klempner **male**
3. Köchin **female**
4. Elektrikerin **female**
5. Arzt **male**
6. Tischlerin **female**
7. Landwirt **male**
8. Programiererin **female**
9. Lehrerin **female**
10. Krankenpfleger **male**

C You will hear two short sentences. Write them down. (5 points)

1. Ich arbeite gern. **Ich arbeite gern.**
2. Wo arbeitest du? **Wo arbeitest du?**

Unit 9

A You will hear the names of certain foods and beverages. Below you will see five categories. Place a check mark under the correct category. You will use some categories twice. (8 points)

1. das Eis		**Dessert**
2. die Birne		**Fruit**
3. das Hähnchen		**Meat**
4. die Milch		**Beverage**
5. der Spinat		**Vegetable**
6. der Apfel		**Fruit**
7. die Kekse		**Dessert**
8. das Mineralwasser		**Beverage**

B You will hear menus for the three meals of the day. Decide whether you hear a traditional breakfast menu, a lunch menu, or a dinner/supper menu. (3 points)

1. Es gibt Hühnerfrikassee, Kartoffeln, grüne Bohnen und Spinat.	**Mittagessen**
2. Es gibt Salat, Brot und Tomatensuppe.	**Abendessen**
3. Es gibt Toastbrot, Marmelade, Butter und Orangensaft.	**Frühstück**

C You will hear a list of table items. Circle the letter of the correct picture. (9 points)

1. das Salz	**B**
2. das Messer	**C**
3. die Tasse	**C**
4. die Untertasse	**A**
5. der Teller	**B**
6. die Serviette	**A**
7. das Glas	**C**
8. die Tischdecke	**B**
9. der Löffel	**A**

Unit 10

A You will hear a description of a painting. Place a check mark in the column of the artist who created it. (6 points)

1. an animal with long ears .... **Dürer**
2. big horses and a brightly colored background .... **Marc**
3. a landscape after a storm .... **Friedrich**
4. a child holding a cat .... **Votteler**
5. people walking along a street .... **Kirchner**
6. a box of dried soil .... **Dietz**

B You will hear the names of four famous artists. Select the description of the style used by that person. Select your answers using the letter A, B, C, or D. (4 points)

1. Caspar David Friedrich .... **C**
2. Albrecht Dürer .... **A**
3. Franz Marc .... **B**
4. Ernst Ludwig Kirchner .... **D**

C You will hear four different kinds of artwork. Select the letter of the person most closely associated with each one. (4 points)

1. pictures showing fantasy and charm .... **D**
2. pictures showing bold colors and vivid outlines .... **A**
3. pictures showing exact detail .... **B**
4. pictures showing northern landscapes .... **C**

D Write down the words you hear. (6 points)

1. Ich zeichne ein Bild. .... **Ich zeichne ein Bild.**
2. Künstler .... **Künstler**
3. Kunst .... **Kunst**
4. Leben .... **Leben**
5. kurz .... **kurz**
6. lang .... **lang**

Unit

A

Listen and identify each part of the body you hear by writing the corresponding letter on the line. (8 points)

1. der Mund   **C**
2. das Haar   **F**
3. die Schulter   **I**
4. die Brust   **J**
5. das Gesicht   **E**
6. der Bauch   **L**
7. der Kopf   **G**
8. die Hand   **M**
9. das Bein   **N**
10. das Knie   **O**
11. der Fuß   **P**
12. der Hals   **H**
13. die Stirn   **A**
14. das Ohr   **B**
15. der Ellenbogen   **K**
16. die Lippe   **D**

B

You will hear the words for four parts of the body. Each item consists of a definite article and a noun. Write each German article and noun. (4 points)

1. das Auge   **das Auge**
2. das Kinn   **das Kinn**
3. die Nase   **die Nase**
4. der Zahn   **der Zahn**

C

You will hear three words. Write the opposite of each word. (3 points)

1. ungesund   **gesund**
2. krank   **wohl**
3. glücklich   **traurig**

D You will hear five questions. Circle the letter of the correct response. (5 points)

1. Wie geht's? **A**
2. Was hast du? **B**
3. Ist Claudia heute krank? **A**
4. Wie fühlst du dich? **B**
5. Bist du traurig? **B**

Unit 12

A **Listen and circle the letter of the correct clothing picture. (8 points)**

1. der Bademantel — **B**
2. das Kleid — **A**
3. der Pullover — **C**
4. die Socken — **A**
5. der Mantel — **B**
6. der Rock — **A**
7. der Anzug — **C**
8. die Jacke — **C**

B **You will hear six sentences. On your answer sheet you will have a question relating to each one and three choices of answers. Answer each question by circling the letter of the correct answer. (6 points)**

1. Warte mal! Ich gehe mit! — **C**
2. Ich reise bald in die Schweiz. — **A**
3. Vergiss nicht deinen Skianzug! — **B**
4. Ich gehe heute in ein Konzert. — **A**
5. Ich hole zuerst meine Jacke. — **B**
6. Ich packe meinen Koffer. — **C**

C **You will hear four articles of clothing or accessories. Pick the situation or time when each is appropriate. (4 points)**

1. Schlafanzug — **B**
2. Mantel — **A**
3. Handchuhe — **C**
4. Gürtel — **C**

D **You will hear two questions. Write a short answer in German to each. (2 points)**

Answers will vary, but may include:

1. Was hast du an? — **ein Kleid, (einen) Anzug, eine Hose, ein Hemd**
2. Wie ist der Mantel? — **schön, groß, klein**

Unit 13

A
You will hear eight times of day. Write down the numerical equivalent of what you hear. (8 points)

1. Es ist Viertel vor neun.   **8:45**
2. Es ist Mittag.   **12:00 noon**
3. Es ist ein Uhr.   **1:00**
4. Es ist halb acht.   **7:30**
5. Es ist sechs Uhr fünf.   **6:05**
6. Es ist Viertel nach zehn.   **10:15**
7. Es ist Mitternacht.   **12:00 midnight**
8. Es ist halb zwölf.   **11:30**

B
You will hear four colors. Identify each one by circling the letter of the correct translation. (4 points)

1. weiß   **B**
2. blau   **C**
3. braun   **B**
4. gelb   **A**

C
You will hear four questions. Answer each by circling the letter of the correct response. (4 points)

1. Welche Farbe hat der Elefant?   **B**
2. Welche Farben haben die Tiger?   **A**
3. Um wie viel Uhr ist das Picknick?   **C**
4. Ist es Mittag?   **C**

D
You will hear two questions. Write out a complete answer to both. (4 points)

1. Wie viel Uhr ist es?   **Es ist . . .** *Answers will vary.*
2. Welche Farbe hat das Gras?   **Das Gras ist grün.**

Unit 14

A You will hear the first names of three composers. Put a check mark in the column with the last name of each composer. (3 points)

1. Wolfgang Amadeus . . .   **Mozart**

2. Ludwig van . . .   **Beethoven**

3. Johann Sebastian . . .   **Bach**

B You will hear seven words or names. Identify each one by circling the letter of the correct description. (7 points)

1. Bonn   **A**

2. *Fidelio*   **B**

3. *St. Matthew Passion*   **C**

4. *The Pastoral*   **C**

5. *Six Brandenburg Concertos*   **B**

6. Salzburg   **A**

7. *Die Zauberflöte*   **A**

C You will hear the names of three works. Place a check mark in the column for the appropriate style of each work. (3 points)

1. *Eine Kleine Nachtmusik* (A Little Night Music)   **Classical**

2. *Die Sechste Sinfonie* (The Sixth Symphony)   **Romantic**

3. *Sechs Brandenburgische Konzerte* (Six Brandenburg Concertos)   **Baroque**

D You will hear names from the world of contemporary music. Determine whether each name refers to A (a singer) or B (a musical group). (7 points)

1. Peter Licht   **A**

2. *Fettes Brot*   **B**

3. Thomas Quasthoff   **A**

4. *Die Dissidenten*   **B**

5. *Silbermond*   **B**

6. Stefanie Hertl   **A**

7. *Clepsydra*   **B**

Unit 15

A
You will hear five weather reports. On your paper you have two categories of weather. Place a check mark in the correct column. (5 points)

1. Es blitzt. **B**
2. Es regnet. **B**
3. Es ist warm. **A**
4. Die Sonne scheint. **A**
5. Es donnert. **B**

B
You will hear four words or expressions. Write the English meaning of each. (4 points)

1. Jahreszeit **season**
2. heiß **hot**
3. Wetter **weather**
4. schlecht **bad**

C
You will hear five sentences. Choose the logical association or response for each. (5 points)

1. Es ist sehr sonnig. **B**
2. Es ist sehr kalt. **A**
3. Es regnet. **B**
4. Wir haben Winter. **B**
5. Wir haben Frühling. **A**

D
You will hear two questions. Answer each one in a complete sentence in German. (6 points)

1. Welche Jahreszeit haben wir? **Wir haben Winter (Sommer, Frühling, Herbst).**
2. Wie ist das Wetter im Sommer? **Es ist heiß.**

Unit **16**

A You will hear dates. Write down each one in number form. Remember that the day always goes before the month. (3 points)

1. der achte Juni **8.6.**
2. der vierzehnte Mai **14.5.**
3. der erste April **1.4.**
4. der dritte Oktober **3.10.**
5. der einundzwanzigste März **21.3.**
6. der dreißigste November **30.11.**

B You will hear eight German words. Identify each one by circling the letter of the correct answer. (8 points)

1. der Schultag **A**
2. morgen **B**
3. der Monat **A**
4. Freitag **C**
5. gestern **B**
6. übermorgen **B**
7. Donnerstag **C**
8. Januar **A**

C You will hear seven questions. Circle the letter of the correct answer. (7 points)

1. Was hast du heute? **B**
2. Welches Datum haben wir heute? **A**
3. Ist heute Mittwoch? **A**
4. Wann ist die Englischarbeit? **B**
5. Was ist Juli? **B**
6. Wann ist der Feiertag? **A**
7. Was ist Donnerstag? **B**

D Write a short answer in German to each question. (2 points)

1. Welcher Tag ist heute? *Answers will vary.*
2. Wann hast du Geburtstag? *Answers will vary.*

Unit 17

A

Match the sounds you hear with the words you see. You will hear the German titles of literary works, labeled A through F. Match each title you hear with the words. Write the appropriate letter in the space provided. (6 points)

A. *Maria Stuart*

B. *Nussknacker und Mausekönig*

C. *Styx*

D. *Faust*

E. *Der geteilte Himmel*

F. *Landaufenthalt*

1. C

2. E

3. A

4. F

5. B

6. D

B

You will hear six clues as to the identity of six great authors. They will be labeled A through F. Write the letter of each clue next to the name it matches. (6 points)

A. This man wrote many poems and historical plays.

B. This woman expressed her sorrow for victims of abuse.

C. This man was a statesman and scientist as well as a writer.

D. This woman wants people and governments to respect each other.

E. This man was a musician as well as a storyteller.

F. This woman was an artist as well as poet.

1. B

2. D

3. A

4. C

5. F

6. E

C

You will hear the names of four works. What kind of literary work is each? Place a check mark in the correct column. (4 points)

1. *Faust* — **Play**

2. *Nussknacker und Mausekönig* — **Story**

3. *Hebräische Balladen* — **Poetry**

4. *Der geteilte Himmel* — **Novel**

D

You will hear the names of four places. Which place is associated with each author? Place a check mark in the column of the correct author. (4 points)

1. Berlin — **Elsa Lasker-Schüler**

2. Königsberg — **Hoffmann**

3. Frankfurt — **Goehte**

4. Marbach — **Schiller**

Check-up Listening Activities
Answer Key

Teacher's Guide

Unit 18

A You will hear five nouns in German. Circle the letter of the correct association. (5 points)

1. der Fußball   **C**

2. das Museum   **A**

3. der Strand   **B**

4. die Musik   **C**

5. das Buch   **A**

B You will hear six questions. Each one has three choices of replies. Circle the letter of the correct response. (6 points)

1. Wohin gehst du?   **A**

2. Was machst du heute?   **A**

3. Was ist da los?   **B**

4. Willst du mitkommen?   **C**

5. Gehst du heute Abend auf die Party?   **B**

6. Gibt es da Musik?   **A**

C You will hear the beginning of five sentences. Choose the letter of the best completion. (5 points)

1. Ich gehe . . .   **B**

2. Das Dürerfest findet diese Woche . . .   **A**

3. Ich fahre gern . . .   **C**

4. Ich tanze . . .   **B**

5. Ich lese . . .   **C**

D You will hear two questions. Answer each one in a complete sentence. *Auf Deutsch, bitte!* (4 points)

1. Welche Sportart treibst du?   *Answers will vary.*

2. Was machst du gern?   *Answers will vary.*

Unit 19

A
You will hear eight words. Circle the letter of the correct English equivalent. (8 points)

1. der Verkäufer   **C**
2. die Kassiererin   **A**
3. das Geld   **B**
4. die Kundin   **C**
5. billig   **C**
6. die Pfirsiche   **A**
7. kaufen   **B**
8. Geschäft   **C**

B
You will hear five words in German. Write each one down. Be sure to include the definite article. (5 points)

1. der Euro   **der Euro**
2. das Kleingeld   **das Kleingeld**
3. der Kunde   **der Kunde**
4. die Kasse   **die Kasse**
5. der Preis   **der Preis**

C
You will hear five questions or statements. Circle the letter of the best reply. (5 points)

1. Wohin gehst du?   **C**
2. Was kaufst du auf dem Markt?   **B**
3. Was darf es sein?   **A**
4. Sind die Tomaten billig?   **C**
5. Noch etwas?   **B**

D
You will hear two questions. Answer each in a complete sentence in German. (2 points)

1. Ist die CD teuer?   *Answers will vary.*
2. Wie viel kostet die CD?   *Answers will vary.*

Unit 20

A

You will hear six phrases. Circle the letter of the correct English equivalent. (6 points)

1. mit dem Zug   **A**
2. Ich fliege.   **B**
3. auf dem Flughafen   **A**
4. bei der Passkontrolle   **C**
5. eine Rückfahrkarte   **B**
6. zweite Klasse   **B**

B

You will hear six words with their definite articles. Write down each word including *der, die,* or *das.* (6 points)

1. der Koffer   **der Koffer**
2. der Fahrplan   **der Fahrplan**
3. der Reisende   **der Reisende**
4. der Schalter   **der Schalter**
5. die Angestellte   **die Angestellte**
6. das Auto   **das Auto**

C

You will hear five questions. Circle the letter of the best reply. (5 points)

1. Wo steht das Flugzeug?   **C**
2. Um wie viel Uhr fährt der nächste Zug nach Berlin?   **A**
3. Wie komme ich zum Hotel Krone?   **B**
4. Wo ist die Fahrkarte?   **A**
5. Ist das ein Schiff?   **A**

D

You will hear three questions. Answer each in a complete sentence in German. (3 points)

1. Wie reist du?   *Answers will vary.*
2. Wo ist der Koffer?   *Answers will vary.*
3. Um wie viel Uhr fährt der Bus? *Answers will vary.*